I0876099

What is Lutheran?

Lutheran Theology
German Perspectives and Positions
Vol. 1

VELKD

LUTHERISCHER WELTBUND
DEUTSCHES NATIONALKOMITEE

What is Lutheran?

Lutheran Theology, Worship, Church Law, Congregations, Ecumenism in brief

Published on behalf of the United Evangelical Lutheran Church of Germany (VELKD) with the German National Committee of the Lutheran World Federation (GNC/LWF) by Henrike Müller und Florian Hübner

Translated by Neville Williamson

EVANGELISCHE VERLAGSANSTALT
Leipzig

Bibliographic information published by the Deutsche Nationalbibliothek
The Deutsche Nationalbibliothek lists this publication in the Deutsche Nationalbibliographie; detailed bibliographic data are available on the Internet at http://dnb.dnb.de.

Printed in Germany

This book is printed on ageing resistant paper.

Cover: Kai-Michael Gustmann, Leipzig
Typesetting: Steffi Glauche, Leipzig
Printing and Binding: Hubert & Co., Göttingen

ISBN 978-3-374-05913-3
www.eva-leipzig.de

Foreword

In the 21st century, Lutheran theology is globalised theology. Just as the Lutheran communion has spread into all parts of the world, so too is theology now practised in a variety of linguistic and cultural contexts. International theological exchange and transcultural learning are therefore of decisive significance for a worldwide church.

For this reason, after the Reformation anniversary in 2017, the United Evangelical Lutheran Church of Germany (VELKD), together with the German National Committee of the Lutheran World Federation (GNC/LWF), has initiated a new series of books in English, the first volume of which you are holding in your hand. These texts were originally published in German and have now been translated into English. The texts and opinions originating from the German-speaking context are intended to be a contribution to theological exchange and the reflection of Lutheran theology beyond national and language boundaries. In this way, the articles do not claim universal validity, but represent one voice among many in the concert of world Christianity.

The series begins with a collection of five texts published in 2017/2018 by the VELKD in German as booklets in connection with the 500th anniversary and commemoration of the Reformation. Five core themes of Protestant theology and the church are presented from a Lutheran perspective and published together here for the first time in one volume: »Given for You. Lutheran Theology« (Michael Roth), »Descent and Ascent. On Lutheran Worship« (Christian Lehnert), »Church for the People. Guidelines for Protestant Parish Work« (Martin Kumlehn), »Fellowship in Practice. Ecumenism from a Lutheran Perspective« (Bernd Oberdorfer) and »The Church and Its Law« (Hendrik Munsonius). The texts are short and compact, as were the original VELKD booklets in a handy pocket format, combining theological reflection with easy-to-understand information. They are suitable not only for theologians from university, church and parish background, but also for interested lay people. Since the individual booklets were written by different authors, they each have a particular style and approach to the topic concerned.

We hope that these texts will offer an international readership interesting, stimulating and theologically well-founded insights into these central subjects. For the Lutheran churches in Germany, this book also indicates how important it is that they are embedded in the worldwide context of ecumenism, and particularly Lutheranism.

Hanover/Schwerin, October 2018

Gerhard Ulrich,
Presiding Bishop of the VELKD and Chairperson of the GNC/LWF

Table of Contents

Michael Roth

Given for you: Lutheran Theology

Christian Lehnert

Descent and Ascent: On Lutheran Worship

Michael Roth

Given for You

Lutheran Theology

1. Introduction: A booklet on accounting for faith

A comeback for religion?

To some contemporaries, religion seems to be a relic of old, pre-scientific and pre-enlightened times, something that should by rights have no place in the modern world. Therefore, even a few years ago, the so-called theory of secularisation was the centre of heated debate, claiming that religion will disappear from the modern, secular world. It forecast that it was only a question of time before religion would disappear completely from the modern world.

This picture has changed significantly in the last few years. From a range of different perspectives it has been pointed out that the resurgence of religion in modern culture clearly shows that religion also has its legitimate place there. »Comeback of religion« is the slogan often employed. In his world-famous book »The Clash of Civilizations« the Harvard political scientist Samuel P. Huntington wrote: »In the modern world, religion plays a central, perhaps even the central role that motivates and mobilizes people.« In the meanwhile, terms used are »respiritualisation« (Matthias Horx), »de-secularisation« (Peter L. Berger) or a »post-secular society« (Jürgen Habermas).

But what is religion?

Now it is possible to be sceptical in welcoming the renaissance of religion, or at least be cautious about measuring all such phenomena prematurely with the same yardstick. Even if we agree that a there is real evidence of a renaissance of religion, that does not necessarily mean that religion and modernity are compatible. It could be that anti-modern forces are rearing their heads for the last time before disappearing completely, in a last major offensive before surrendering. Religion could also be the shadow of reason, the monster produced by the »Sleep of Reason« in the painting by Francisco de Goya. And there is another question. What about other trends which are also described by sociologists, the ones that relativize the renaissance of religion, such as the progressively increasing secularisation and a habitual atheism that is no longer militant, but lives a life without God as a matter of course without feeling that anything is missing? Above all, when speaking of the »comeback of religion«, one should look closely into the phenomena which are all subsumed under the label of »religion«. What exactly is enjoying a comeback? Does it warrant the title of »religion« or should it be classified as diffuse religiosity in distinction to religion as such? Can one say that lighting a joss stick is really equivalent to a trusting confidence which lasts a lifetime? To speak of transcendental energies or a cosmic spirit, or to take part in a religious event like the »Kirchentag« or World Youth Day, can that already be the foundation of daily religious practice?

Educated religion?

The phenomenon of »resurgence of religion« leads to another issue, namely the resurgence of fundamentalist forms of religion. This tendency is also evident in Christianity. It is not uncommon for faith to be seen in opposition to reason; Christian fundamentalism demands that the Bible should not be the object of rational understanding, but of obedience that renounces reason. The rejection of modernity in these circles is expressed, for example, by the demand that the theory of evolution should be replaced in the school curriculum by the theory of »intelligent design«. Like the spiritualisation of religion, fundamentalist Christianity also thrives at the expense of traditional religion.

Spiritualisation and fundamentalisation present themselves to us as two »solutions« in determining the relationship between modernity and religion – and thus the relationship between faith and reason. Evaporation of religion on the one hand, farewell to modernity on the other, or to put it another way: abandonment of the claim to truth on the one hand and fundamentalist claim to truth on the other. Is there a third way?

Purpose of this booklet: Theological reflection on the faith and its foundations

This booklet is an attempt to account for the faith – to reflect on the form and manifestation of the Christian faith to which the Lutheran Church is committed. Such reflected accountability seems to be typical for Christianity as a whole, which by means of theology has always taken care to account for faith in a scientific discipline.

The term »theology« does not come from the Bible, but from Greek antiquity, and means in the original sense of the word »speaking about God«, that is to say, singing and reciting stories about gods, first of all orally and later in writing. In this way, Plato made use of the term theology, albeit critically. Unlike Plato, Aristotle uses the term theology not to refer to the narrating of stories about the gods, but rather to the philosophical question about God, seeking to reveal through rational thinking how the myths transport falsehood in their tales of God. Christianity has adopted the term »theology«, using it as a term for the considered reflection on the Christian faith. This means that it is committed to both elements in the concept of theology: reference to history on the one hand and reasonable accountability on the other. Since the founding of universities in the Middle Ages, theology, this reflection on the Christian faith, has become one of the established university disciplines (alongside medicine, jurisprudence and philosophy).

It is to be hoped that this booklet will provide an understanding of what faith is all about: not a rigid belief in statements about the world and God, but a »life perspective« empowering people to conduct their daily life in the present, rather than remaining fixated in an unresolved past, or losing themselves in a fantasized future. That can succeed simply by trust in this promise: »Take and eat, it is given for you!«

Method and structure of the booklet

First of all, we want to look closely into the phenomenon of religious faith. The central question here is »What is faith?« In a second step we shall focus on the central contents of the faith. And thirdly, we want to investigate Christian life.

2. Faith in practice

How can one talk about God?

It is by no means the case that people are not interested in questions about the existence of God. Therefore, talking about God is not condemned to failure from the start. But the main point is, in what way should one talk about God?

The reason why it is not easy to talk about God is that people associate very different interests with conversations about God. Some people want to talk about God in an abstract fashion, speculating on the reasons behind the world, while others can only talk about God from a position of existential concern. For them, speaking about God always has to do with liberation and hope in their own lives. This difference became clear in a conversation which I overheard while travelling in an Intercity train from Bonn to Erfurt.

Conversation on the train

The conversation took place between two young men who obviously knew each other well. At any rate they were aware that one of them regarded himself as an atheist, while the other was a professing believer. I did not gather anything about the first part of their conversation but I pricked up my ears when I heard one of them say, »No, I am indeed an atheist but I really enjoy arguing with believers about the existence of God.« He was sitting quite relaxed with crossed legs, looking at his opposite number in a friendly and expectant way. Then he went on cheerfully: »Up to now, I haven't heard any convincing arguments for his existence. Above all, when you look at all the suffering and injustice in the world, it seems to me quite absurd to believe in the existence of a good and righteous God.« The other man looked at him uncertainly. He was obviously reluctant to enter into the discussion his friend had opened, and very clearly did not appear to share his enthusiasm. »What's the matter?« said the latter. »You really don't have to worry. I would really like to argue with you about the existence of God, exchanging the reasons that speak in favour of his existence or against it. And you ought to enjoy it, too – after all, you do believe that God exists. Do your best to convince me he exists. I'm looking forward to hearing what you can bring forward.« After thinking for some time, the other man answered: »I am not really interested in wondering whether God exists. That is not my question.« Now it was the turn of the avowed atheist to be consternated: »All right, but if you are so convinced of God's existence that you do not even call it into question, then you should not find it difficult to present some arguments in favour of it.« Then he was given an unexpected answer: »You want to argue about God just as you would argue about the existence of the yeti. But I can't talk about God in the same sort of way!« When asked why not, the one who was being questioned about his faith replied: »Because it's not the same thing – you want to talk about God without getting involved personally! I can't do that!«

Belief in God and belief that a yeti exists

This conversation between the self-confessed atheist and the man who professed his religion makes it clear why it is often so difficult even to start a conversation about God. One does indeed have the feeling that many people want to talk about

God's existence in the same way as they would talk about the existence of a yeti in the Himalayas. You discuss the existence of a yeti by considering what reasons speak in favour of its existence and what grounds there are for refusing to believe it. But if you were to speak about God in a similar way, you would take leave of the existential dimension which is essential for the language of faith. Does talking about God not entail more than just discussing a theistic object whose existence we either do or do not believe to be true? Is it even possible to talk about God without talking about oneself and one's own hopes and expectations?

Religious talk of God

It would be a misunderstanding of religious faith to see it as »being convinced« of the existence of God. Religious talk about God is quite different from the belief in the existence of a yeti, not only by content, but also by category. You cannot have a debate on faith by arguing about God as an object, as one might argue about the existence of a yeti-object. A dispute between people supporting the hypothesis of the existence of a yeti and the adversaries of such a hypothesis is quite a different matter to the dispute between believers and sceptics. This dispute does not concern theoretical knowledge about a particular being, but rather the conflict between differing ways of life.

What is faith?

If religious belief is distinct from »being convinced« of God's existence, and therefore from theoretical knowledge about a particular object, then the question arises: what is faith? We want to try to put together some aspects of faith which help us to answer that question.

Different usage of the term »belief«

First we should take a look at the everyday language use of the term »belief«. Ordinarily, we use the term »belief« in the sense of »accepting the truth« of a statement, meaning »I believe this, that and the other«. I might be using the word in this sense, for example, when I say »I believe the table is two metres long«. But although the concept of »belief« is commonly used in this sense of »accepting the truth«, that is not the only way it is used. When I say »I believe you«, then I am using the word in a completely different way.

In this case, I mean »believe« in the sense of »trust«. It is important to distinguish between the use of the concept of »belief« in the sense of trust (»I believe you«) and the use of the same word to mean »accepting as true« (»I believe that …«). In many languages different words exist for these two different concepts, so that English, for example, makes the distinction between »belief« and »faith«.

Belief as trust

When the reaction to God's promise in Christ is described as »belief«, then the term is not used in the sense of »accepting the truth« of a statement, but rather in the sense of trust (»faith«). This is of great importance, because otherwise it is not clear what Christianity is. It may lead to a distorted notion of what it means to be a Christian. It is not the essence of Christianity to be convinced of certain propositions which are denied by others, but rather to trust in them in a certain way.

The Reformation understanding of faith

In the Reformation tradition, there is a particular emphasis on the character of belief as trust (*fiducia*). Thus, in the Large Catechism, Luther refers to faith as a »trust of the heart« directed toward Christ. When Luther formulates, »Faith remains purely and simply attached to the word alone, turns its gaze not away, nor looks for something else«,[1] then it is clear that faith is understood as a movement shaping and determining one's entire life – in all its facets. This is unmistakably clear in Luther's exposition of the first commandment in the Large Catechism: »To have a God is nothing else than to trust and believe Him from the [whole] heart; as I have often said, that the confidence and faith of the heart alone make both God and an idol. If your faith and trust be right, then is your God also true; and, on the other hand, if your trust be false and wrong, then you have not the true God; for these two belong together, faith and God. That now, I say, upon which you set your heart and put your trust is properly your God.« Thus, Luther understands faith as the fulfilment of the first commandment; because he trusts in God's promise »I am the Lord, your God!« In the Large Catechism, Luther interprets this promise as follows: »I, yes I, will give you enough and help you out of every need; only let not your heart cleave to or rest in any other.« The appropriate response to such

1 »Der glawb hanget alleyn dem wort blos und lautter an, wendet die augen nicht darvon, sihet keyn ander ding an« Translation: Williamson.

a promise is not to »know« it, to »recognize« it or »be convinced it is true«, but to make it effective in one's life by a trusting attitude. In a nutshell, the appropriate response to God's promise is to confide in him with one's whole being, or in a single word: trust. Thus, God's promise and human trust belong together.

Faith and existence

Now it has become abundantly clear that declared belief is not about some more or less irrelevant objective facts that one considers to be true, but about one's own existence. Therefore, faith is not about questions concerning particular facts in the world. Questions such as whether the town of Kiel lies to the north or to the south of Hamburg, or whether or not rabbits are ruminant animals. Those are not existential questions, but simply matters of fact. Faith, on the other hand, is not about factual issues, but about questions of one's own existence. Faith is also not about individual questions concerning the world of experience as a whole, for example the question of how far away the moon is from the Earth, or whether the Earth was created in six days or six million years. Such questions also only deal with the position of the Earth in the planetary system or its age, they are not existential questions. Faith deals with the question: »Who am I?«

Requirement of faith

If the Christian faith is understood as holding certain factual statements to be true, it is in danger of becoming shallow because it is deprived of the existential dimension. Faith is about one's own existence. On the other hand, people who speculate on such questions as to whether or not the world was actually created in six days are not talking about their own existence. They are not making any reference to their self-understanding or to the grounds of their lives and hopes. They are talking about something without taking any risk or getting involved personally. But in this way they remove themselves from the requirement of faith, which does not consist in holding on to some strange statements or hypotheses about the world of experience which are unacceptable to any rational thinking person, but in living a life of trust in God. Faith confronts me with the question: how do you want to live? What is your consolation in life and in death? It does not confront me with the question: do you think it is true that rabbits are ruminants?

Reformation understanding of the belief in creation

Luther's interpretation of the creation may serve as an example of the indissoluble connection between faith and existence: »I believe that God has made me and all creatures; that He has given me my body and soul, eyes, ears, and all my limbs, my reason, and all my senses, and still preserves them; in addition thereto, clothing and shoes, meat and drink, house and homestead, wife and children, fields, cattle, and all my goods; that He provides me richly and daily with all that I need to support this body and life, protects me from all danger and guards me and preserves me from all evil; and all this out of pure, fatherly, divine goodness and mercy, without any merit or worthiness in me; for all which I owe it to Him to thank, praise, serve, and obey Him. This is most certainly true.«

If we take a closer look at the text, it strikes us straightaway that Luther emphasises the presence of the creator and his actions. This emphasis is closely related to a second distinctive feature: when giving his interpretation of the Apostles' Creed, the speaker does not remain distant from his subject, referring in an abstract fashion to »something«; rather he talks about his own person and existence: »I believe that God has made me«, »my body and soul«, »without any merit or worthiness in me«, »for all which I owe it to Him to thank …«. Though the believer does not appear in the text of the Apostolic Creed, which only presents the pure facts (»I believe in God, the Father almighty, creator of heaven and earth«), Luther's interpretation relates these facts to the life of the individual believer.

Existential meaning of the creation statements

Therefore, it would diminish Luther's interpretation if one were only to see in it statements about the world which the person reciting the Creed acknowledges to be true. Rather, it is an expression of an attitude to life that relates to the perceived world in order to find its place within it. Everything obtaining to human life, every sphere of activity which constitutes a person's being, is understood to be a gift of creation. This is also evident in the enumeration of individual gifts of creation, reminiscent of the list language in Old Testament wisdom literature. This is not intended as a designation in scientific accuracy. It may be seen as a conscious selection; the series of items leaves gaps which can be individually filled by the imagination of anyone who recites or hears the text. The people who join in speaking the Creed are invited to express themselves as subjects in the perceived world – each in a particular way and at a specific place.

These statements are not statements about the world, but about *my own* place in the world, they are not motivated cosmologically but existentially. The believer who praises the world as God's creation is making a statement about his place in the world and the world as the place where he lives. The world is described as a God-granted habitat. The language of the Christian religion does not express theoretical knowledge about the world, but makes statements about human beings in the world: they have been freed by God to live.

Creation faith in contrast to a cosmological theory

The belief in creation is therefore something other than being convinced of the truth of the cosmological statement »God is the originator of the world«. The statement that the world is the product of an uncaused cause is a descriptive statement about the world. I can believe it to be true or false, without stating anything about my own life. Thus, the statement that the world is the product of an uncaused cause lies on the level of belief in the existence of extra-terrestrial life; it is a matter of speculation – whether meaningful or simply transcending the capabilities of human cognition is not the question here. It is therefore not surprising that there are certainly people who are willing to believe the statement that the world owes its existence to an uncaused cause, but have nothing else to do with a religious life. It is not problematic that people are to be found who (merely) believe that the world originates from an unmoved mover, an uncaused cause or the like – no more than that there are people who, on the basis of their observations of the world, consider it likely that a yeti exists in the Himalayas. In religious terms, both positions are unspectacular. However, it does become a problem when such intellectual fantasies about the unmoved mover as the origin of the world are confused with the Christian belief in creation. When the Christian faith speaks about creation, it is not making a purely objective statement about the world (neither about the structures of the world of experience nor about the cause of these structures), isolated from statements about itself.

The predication of the world as creation also poses the question »Who am I?«, which expresses how the speaker leads and interprets his life – but not what theory about the origin of the world he believes in.

Faith as a guideline for life

When we look at the different aspects of belief, one misunderstanding stands out clearly: a widespread misconception about faith is that knowledge related to faith is equivalent to empirical factual knowledge. On the contrary, it should be noted that the word »faith« signifies a certain »conduct of life«, a particular attitude to living. It should be repeated here: Christians are not distinguished by the fact that they are convinced of the truth of statements that others consider to be false, but rather by participating in a certain way of life which determines the course of their entire life. Faith does not entail a particular form of confession, but a particular form of living. Faith means a special kind of awareness of the world, a special kind of conduct in and towards this world.

Faith and talking of God

Faith is a certain attitude to life which cannot avoid speaking about God whenever it expresses itself. The word »God« is inseparable from this context – indeed, the expression »God« really finds its definition in the daily conduct of faith. When there is mention of God in the context of this attitude to life, then he is not something I might speak of purely objectively, isolated from any reference to myself. The use of the term »God« is an expression of a person's own place in the world. The term »God« cannot be perceived and reflected upon in isolation. God is not the name for something which might be considered or discussed on its own, removed from the specific conduct of life and then analysed. Statements employing such words as »here«, »now« or »today« are not related to some kind of factual »here«, »now« or »today«, but rather indicate where and when the speaker sees his own place in the world. In the same way, when talking about faith, statements using the word »God« do not relate to God-facts, which might be understood independently of the concrete use of the words. Talk about God can also not be isolated from this concrete use of the word without being rendered incomprehensible and meaningless, and above all not without losing their significance for the concrete life of the person speaking in prayer. The believer talks about God by speaking about himself, and talks about himself by speaking about God.

Religious faith in contrast to theism and atheism

We have said that faith is something other than the conviction that God exists, but we can obviously not ignore the fact that there really is such conviction. This is the case in rational theism. Rational theism is a theory. It is not a living faith, nor factually a religion. It is therefore necessary to distinguish faith from rational theism, with which it is often confused.

Rational theism is the conviction that a god exists who is almighty, all-wise and all-good and created and sustains the world. Rational theism is a theory claiming to demonstrate that the hypothesis of God's existence provides a better explanation for the observations of the world and its phenomena than the hypothesis of his non-existence. Theism assumes that rational insights can prove the existence of God and it makes use of philosophical, empirical or scientific arguments to this purpose. Atheism has a certain resemblance to rational theism in that it assumes that God is simply a theory to explain the world. Unlike rational theism, atheism assumes that God is not a suitable model to explain reality, either because this hypothesis has been made superfluous by the results of scientific research, or because the problem of theodicy renders this hypothesis unlikely.

Faith is clearly distinct from this rational theism – if faith is understood as a form of life conduct. It is important to realise that the term »God« functions differently in different contexts, and that the meaning is not always and everywhere the same when reference is made to GOD. It makes a difference whether the term »God« is used in rational deliberations on the way the world is experienced or whether it is used in the language of faith.

Confusion of religious faith with theism

The problem with (many) atheistic denials of faith consists in the fact that they confuse faith with theism, suggesting that the differences between believers and non-believers lie in the arguments for and against the existence of God. This is clearly the case with Richard Dawkins, who reduces faith to an attitude of religious persuasion, which is then put to the test and rejected in the light of the scientific criteria. It is obvious that Dawkins confuses (religious) faith with rational theism (that is a theory). But it cannot be the task of theology to defend theism, which is denied by atheism, and not advocated by believers. (Even if theism were to succeed in bringing argumentative proof of the existence of the God it postulates, that would not amount to a proof of the God we talk about in the Christian religion.) If atheists think that they can remove the key religious statements about God from their context and insert them into the grammar used for scientific statements, then they are naturally welcome to do so. However, a theology which sees its purpose in accounting for faith will not assume that such non-existential mental pastimes attempting to explain world phenomena have anything to do with faith, or even form a threat to it.

Talking about God and talking to God

Martin Luther states: »As is the business of tailors to make clothes and cobblers to make shoes, so it is the business of Christians to pray. Prayer is the craft of a Christian.« Prayer is essential for the practice of faith, here it finds its most direct expression – in petition, thanksgiving and lamentation to God and before him. This fact is decisive: faith is not characterised by talking about God (i. e. theorising about God), but by talking to God (i. e. leading a life which reckons with God). In prayer, talking to God, the believer speaks about his life – in the presence of God. He speaks about his life in the presence of the one from whom he expects all that is good. This is the very way in which God *becomes* God. God does not become God simply because his existence is believed to be true and well known, but because he is trusted – when people live with him and in his presence. God is proved true by the way the believer leads his life. And the other way round: confession of God is empty if it does not correspond to the conduct of life. In that sense, faith is »creator of deity«, to quote a term coined by Martin Luther. God can only be defined on the basis of this trust.

Christian understanding of God

The use of the term »God« in the Christian religion cannot be detached from what is expressed in this explanation: the life-giving promise in the encounter with the person of Jesus of Nazareth. The Christian religion does not speak about God in an abstract way, but only with reference to the person liberated by God in Christ. That means that there can be no talk of God without defining a person's place in the world in a certain way. To consider God in faith means to reflect on one's own life, which is determined by the encounter with Jesus of Nazareth as God's Christ. We have established that faith is something other than a theory about an absolute being, but rather a movement of trust based on the encounter with Jesus of Nazareth. The term »God« serves to describe how incomparable, inaccessible and unsurpassable this event is for my life. Christian talk of God cannot be detached from this usage without losing its meaning. One must hold fast to this: in faith, a person does not speak first of God and then of his life, but rather speaks of God by relating the significance of this event in his life, thus describing the incomparability, inaccessibility and unsurpassability of the experience.

Conversation about God as a conversation about one's own life

Now there is no doubt about the kind of conversation a believer can hold with a sceptic: not a conversation about the probability of the existence of an almighty and benevolent being, a theistic object, but a conversation about one's own life, liberated by the encounter with Jesus of Nazareth as the God's Christ. Truth occurs within this encounter. The truth of faith cannot be proved other than in this encounter. The believer cannot produce evidence for belief beyond the bounds of this belief. In order to prove the truth of faith he can repeat Philip's reply to Nathanael: »Come and see!«

Venture of faith

Those who believe do not speak first of God and then of their lives, but rather speak of God by speaking of their lives – and then speak in turn of their own lives by speaking of God. For this reason there is no way of clarifying the existence of God in advance, in order to see whether the Christian's trust and hope are based on a firm foundation.

This also applies in view of the theodicy problem, the question of how the almighty and benevolent God can permit suffering in the world. Over and over again, the believer, too, is profoundly shaken at the existence of evil and suffering in the world, seeing it as a challenge to faith. Because believers cannot solve the theodicy problem, they cannot comply with the request to remove this crucial obstacle to the venture of faith in advance. They can only demonstrate what it means to speak about God in the face of the theodicy problem. But they can also try to provide information about this trust that wrestles with a hidden God, that is confronted with doubts, and is even repeatedly thrust into deep darkness, but nonetheless does not abandon God, but holds him to his liberating promise and cries: »I will not let you go, unless you bless me.«

3. The object of faith: sinful humans and the justifying God

Faith and its contents

In the first chapter we have seen that faith does not mean being convinced of the truth of statements about the world and its possible origins, but rather living a certain kind of life in practice. We have ascertained that faith may be defined as a specific way of perceiving the world and behaving within and towards it. The contents of faith, which will now concern us, are not additions to faith; they are the expression of how faith is to be practised, of how people understand and interpret themselves and their lives. Therefore, these faith themes are not supposed to characterise the world in certain respects. They do not contain »information« about the world, humankind and God, but they enable us to define our place in the world. Thus, specific statements of faith (such as »The world is God's creation«) can only be understood when their existential meaning has been comprehended. It must be clear how such statements affect the interpretation and conduct of life. A human being refers to and interprets his own person by speaking about the contents of faith.

The necessity of religious content

It is not possible to live an abstract religious life. It has more to do with the appropriation of language skills and the understanding of the symbols used by a particular religion: rites, creeds, religious stories, traditions, prayers. It appears that religion cannot be learned without them. It is not viable to make the distinction between personal belief and church affiliation; individual religiosity evidently depends on attachment to the structures of religion. It is not we who shape the contents of faith, but the contents of faith form us. They are not the product of our experience of the world, but they characterise and determine our world experience. The contents offer, as it were, a room which we can enter.

Denominational restriction?

Why is it then a good idea to describe the contents of the faith, as is the case with the written confessions of our church? Does it really matter, what is Lutheran and what is not? Isn't this somewhat small-minded in a society in which religion is no longer of central importance and hardly anyone understands confessional differences? Is it still reasonable to make such efforts at delimitation?

At first glance, one might indeed assume that this is a sign of small-mindedness. At a time when Christianity, and even religion in general, threatens to vanish completely, it may well appear pedantic to delineate and highlight the specifics of a particular Christian denomination, for example Lutheranism, rather than looking out for a form of Christianity that transcends denominational borders and generously overcomes hair-splitting demarcations. But is that really true?

Confessions as key to the Scriptures

It is a common opinion that formulated confessions consist of incomprehensible, restrictive and oblique denominational trivialities that have to be accepted by believers and claim to supplement the message of the man from Nazareth, which was unmistakable, well-wishing and liberating. However, this idea misses the point, or at least does not fit in with the concept which lies behind these confessions. Their intention is not to act as additions to the scriptures, but rather as their grammar book: they claim to show how the scriptures are to be understood and how scriptural concerns are to be expressed without obscurity or falsification. More specifically: for Reformation theology, it is essential to emphasise God's righteousness. God is described as the one who makes such clear and unequivocal promises to humans that they can rely on him and be sure of his salvation. The core of Lutheran doctrine is trust in the divine promise that creates this assurance of salvation – in the midst of life's tensions and temptations. Individual teachings, such as the doctrine of the distinction between Law and Gospel, serve to make it clear how one may speak appropriately about God's promise and its life-giving power. On the other hand, should one attempt to strip Christianity of this denominational garment, allowing it to stand before us in its naked, innocent purity, one consequence becomes apparent: this idea would tend to obscure God's liberating promise and replace it with moralising demands. The promise »Look to Christ, that is how I see you!« is perverted into an injunction to have to do something to make oneself acceptable.

In the next section, we want to reflect on essential articles of the faith.

Luther's Reformation »discovery«

What is »reformatory« in Luther's theology? Among Luther researchers, there is disagreement about the time when Luther discovered God's justification by grace alone (*sola gratia*). In order to assess the content of this Reformation discovery more closely, it is important to determine when it took place. The decisive, public argument between Luther and the representatives of the Roman Church came to a head at the Augsburg hearing before Cardinal Cajetan – that is undisputed. »I do not wish to become a heretic by denying that by which I became a Christian; I would rather die, be burned, banished and damned,«[2] said Luther. For him the discovery of God's promise (*promissio*) with its assurance of salvation is of paramount importance. God gives his trustworthy word. These promises show the concrete manner of Christ's presence – unequivocal

---

[2] »Ich will nicht zu einem Ketzer werden, indem ich dem widerspreche, wodurch ich zu einem Christ geworden bin; eher will ich sterben, verbrannt, vertrieben und verflucht werden.« Translation: Williamson.

and giving surety. A verbal deed of this kind (e. g. »Your sins are forgiven!«), which does not describe but rather constitutes a fact, is called by Luther an »efficacious word« (*verbum efficax*). The new understanding of God's *promissio* determines first and foremost his righteousness. In this way, God is understood as the one who gives his promise to humans so reliably and unequivocally that they can trust in God and be sure of their salvation. All other doctrines in Lutheranism are derived from this; they are intended to express this basic trust and protect it from obfuscations.

Centre of Lutheran teaching

The heart of Lutheran teaching is faith in the divine promise that provides assurance of salvation – in the midst of the tensions and temptations of our lives. In the face of all kinds of questions and problems in all kinds of contexts and places, this doctrine tries to show how one can properly speak of God's promise and its life-giving power. Thus, Lutheran doctrine is not concerned with lifeless material, but with the vibrant and dramatic occurrences involving sinful humans and the justifying God. In order to understand the significance of faith in a human life, Lutheran doctrine is as intriguing and conflict-laden as life itself.

Bondage of the will

Luther, as well as those confessional texts that follow his teaching, considers it crucial that the acceptance of salvation – belief, in the sense of trust – is in no way human work, but solely the work of God. God alone works faith in the believer through the Holy Spirit by the word and the sacraments. Therefore, Luther rejects any cooperation between God's prevenient grace and the consenting action of humans, and contradicts the idea of free will. The external word is not an action which is subsequently ratified by human free will. It is God's self-communication and empowerment. Luther denies that a person is in the least capable of accepting or rejecting the salvation offered. To concede this would, for Luther, endanger nothing less than the assurance of salvation. If salvation were not entirely in God's hands, and if humans were obliged to look to themselves as participators, then uncertainty would creep in. Thus, Luther formulates a confession at the end of his polemic response to Erasmus of Rotterdam: »As to myself, I openly confess, that I should not wish ›Free-will‹ to be granted me, even if it could be so, nor anything else to be left in my own hands, whereby I might endeavour something towards my own salvation. And that, not merely because in so many opposing dangers, and so many assaulting devils, I could not stand and hold it fast, [...] but because, even though there were no dangers, no conflicts, no devils, I should be compelled to labour under a continual uncertainty, and to beat the air only. Nor would my conscience, even if I should live and work to all eternity, ever come to a settled certainty, how much it ought to do in order to satisfy God. [...] But now, since God has put my salvation out of the way of my will, and has taken it under His own, and has promised to save me, not according to my working or manner of life, but according to His own grace and mercy, I rest fully assured and persuaded that He is faithful, and will not lie.«

The doctrine of justification by faith alone

The centre of Lutheran doctrine is faith in God's promised assurance of salvation, the doctrine of justification, which offers a comprehensive presentation of this core issue with regard to the theme of righteousness. For the Lutheran Church, this does not rank as one doctrine among others, but is considered to be the one article of faith by which the Church stands or falls.

In a retrospective of 1545, Luther describes the redefinition of the righteousness of God (*iustitia dei*) as a decisive breakthrough. In this autobiographical review, Luther recalls that he was disturbed by the concept of God's righteousness, because he understood this concept in the philosophical sense, according to which justice consists in meting out reward and punishment in a just way (distributive justice). This understanding of justice was also applied to the notion of the Last Judgment; in medieval times, Christ was envisaged as the Judge with divine majesty, before whom mankind would have to answer for their deeds, and this corresponded well with the philosophical concept of justice. This conception of the divine Judge was the source of Luther's misery: if God proved his righteousness by giving everyone their just deserts, therefore punishing the sinner with eternal damnation, then the sinner – and Luther considered himself to be one – has no chance at the Last Judgment.

Rom 1:16f

Luther's distress was intensified unbearably by a passage in Paul's letter to the Romans: Rom 1:16f. This passage reads, »For I am not ashamed of the gospel; it is the power of God for salvation to everyone who has faith, to the Jew first and also to the Greek. For in it the righteousness of God is revealed through faith for faith; as it is written, ›The one who is righteous will live by faith.‹« These verses cause Luther unbearable distress, because they seem to him to declare the content of the gospel to be that very justice of which he is so afraid, the justice that punishes the sinner. For Luther in his desperation, the gospel does not mitigate the sinner's woes, but rather strengthens them.

A liberating discovery

Luther made his liberating discovery in this very passage of Scripture, Rom 1:17, which revealed to him the true meaning of the expression »the righteousness of God«. This is not the righteousness by which God deals out to everyone their just deserts (thus sending the sinner to eternal damnation), but a righteousness which God bestows upon humans (without their own contribution). Righteousness is therefore to be understood as something effected by God, in the sense of: making righteous. God's righteousness is a gift of God which makes people righteous, even though they are not so of their own doing.

The doctrine of distinction between law and gospel

The prerequisite of assurance is unambiguity. The gospel as promise (*promissio*), as a pure promise and unconditional gift, must be distinguished from of any kind of demand on people. If Luther sees it as the decisive breakthrough in his thinking that he understood the concept of »the righteousness of God«

as an undeserved gift to humanity, then it is not surprising that he refers in a different context to the distinction between law and gospel as the decisive breakthrough of his thinking. He makes it clear that his discovery of the »righteousness of God« coincided with his discovery of the distinction between law and gospel: »I lacked nothing before this except that I made no distinction between the law and the gospel. I regarded both as the same thing and held that there was no difference between Christ and Moses except the times in which they lived and their degrees of perfection. But when I discovered the proper distinction – namely, that the law is one thing and the gospel is another – I made myself free.« Luther differentiates between the promise (given in Christ) and the assurance (gospel) granted to humankind without any preconditions – as a free gift – and the commandments given by Moses (law). The distinction is necessary in order to differentiate between God's gift and his demands on humankind. God grants his righteousness by justifying the sinner, not by justifying the person who has obeyed the commandments of his law. The insight into the distinction between law (»You shall ...«) and gospel (»given to you«) is of prime importance, for Luther emphasises with this distinction that God's acceptance is not bound to any requirements or preconditions which people have to fulfil in advance. The gift of acceptance by God and his demands on humans are not to be confused by linking the free gift with the demand and making it a part of it: »You should unravel these two words and put each in its due place.«

Unconditional acceptance

When Luther distinguishes between law and gospel, he wants to make it clear that the acceptance by God is not of a kind that takes a look at a person and finds something there which necessitates such acceptance. In short: the acceptance is not founded in a person's (moral) quality. A person »finds nothing in himself whereby he could be justified«. The self-centred human is not accepted by God, because there is a part of him or her which is not affected by sinful selfishness. Humans are also not accepted by God because of the fact that they are prepared to change their ways in future (upfront acceptance, as it were). For Luther, the unconditional acceptance can only be fully understood by bearing in mind that the gospel is distinct from the law and its commandments: the promise (»given to you«) is independent of every »you shall …« of the law. To express it in relation to the concept of the righteousness of God: through his promise given in the gospel, God justifies people who are unable to justify themselves in their own strength. The doctrine of law and gospel represents the strictest possible denial of self-redemption through ethical efforts.

Humanity: righteous and sinful at the same time

According to Lutheran understanding, a human being is at once righteous and a sinner (*simul iustus et peccator*). Christians remain sinners as well. Therefore, it is crucial for Luther that our righteousness remains the »alien righteousness« (*iustitia aliena*) through Christ. It is not because of our quality, but in the light of Christ, that we are »justified« by God. »Look to Christ, that is how I see you!« Righteousness is thus not a human quality, but founded in God's sight.

Although humans continue to sin, the Reformation tradition by no means denies that justification also has a transformative power. Nevertheless, it should be noted that justification is not based on this new life of the Christian. It is therefore Luther's intention to state unequivocally that justification is founded entirely in the righteousness of Christ. Assurance of salvation through faith stands on this ground alone. »No one ascends into heaven but he who descended from heaven, the Son of man (John 3:13). In his skin and on his back we too must ascend.«

God both hidden and revealed

The talk of God's promise of salvation does not overlook the needs of the world, nor does it ignore the situation of temptation. With reference to negative experiences, the most painful of which is the experience of inability to grasp the faith, Lutheran tradition speaks of the hidden God (*deus absconditus*) and of God's hidden presence. Luther states that this God »is not preached, not revealed, not offered, not worshiped. To the extent, therefore, that God hides himself and his wills to be unknown to us, it is no business of ours. For here the saying truly applies, ›Things above us are no business of ours.‹« When Luther speaks of the hidden God, it is not because he feels the need to speak of further aspects of God, but there are experiences that stand in contradiction to God's promise and are to be taken seriously. The talk of God's hiddenness is not one component in a speculative system, but the expression of a human self-understanding that trusts in God's promise even in the face of contradictory experiences. The concept of hiddenness allows one to hold fast to the symbol of God's omnipotence. Luther does not deny that pain and suffering are also God's work. But he does not set these experiences in opposition to God's promise, but rather expresses by »hiddenness« human outrage, disappointment and incomprehension. In that sense, talk of the hidden God leads to lamentations. Luther says one should »make its way to God against God and pray to Him«, to progress from the God hidden in his will and works to the God who has given his certain promise in Jesus Christ.

In this way, talk of the hidden God ultimately refers for Luther to God's unequivocal word: his promise in the life and death of the man Jesus of Nazareth. »No one will taste the Godhead other than how he wishes to be tasted. He wishes to be seen in the humanity of Christ, and if you do not find the Godhead in this way, you will never find rest. Therefore, just let others speculate and speak of contemplation, of their yearning for God and a foretaste of eternal life, and how spiritual souls begin a contemplative life. But you shall not come to know God that way. However great and mighty he may be – you shall start here, touch him and say first of all, ›I know of no other God than the one given for me in Christ.‹«[3]

---

3 »Niemand wird die Gottheit anders schmecken, als wie sie geschmeckt sein will. Sie will in der Menschheit Christi betrachtet werden, und wenn du die Gottheit nicht auf diese Weise findest, wirst du nimmermehr Ruhe haben. Darum lass die anderen nur spekulieren und von der Beschaulichkeit reden, wie alles mit Gott buhle und einen Vorgeschmack des ewigen Lebens gebe, und wie die geistlichen Seelen ein beschauliches Leben anfangen. Aber du lerne mir Gott nicht auf diese Weise kennen.

The Bible as a source of faith

The Bible is the source of faith and foundation of the Lutheran churches. God's word is bound to the outward form of Scripture. Luther puts it in this way: »Christ has two witnesses to his birth and his realm. The one is Scripture, the word comprehended in the letters of the alphabet. The other is the voice or the words proclaimed by mouth.«

Speaking out against enthusiasts, Luther refers to the external, physical texts. »Therefore we should and must insist that God does not want to deal with us human beings, except by means of his external Word and sacrament. Everything that boasts of being from the Spirit apart from such a Word and sacrament is of the devil.« That is exactly why every kind of arbitrariness is avoided, because »God gives no one his Spirit or grace apart from the external Word which goes before«. Thus, for Luther both things apply: on the one hand, the understanding of Scripture is not at our disposal; the Holy Spirit is essential, if Scripture is to become the interpreter of my life, that is to say, God must be at work. On the other hand, the Holy Spirit does his work by means of the outward form of scriptural texts; for God has bound himself to this word.

Lass ihn sein, wie groß und mächtig er sein mag – beginne du hier und rühre ihn an und sag' zuallererst: ›Ich weiß von keinem anderen Gott als dem, der in Christus für mich gegeben ist‹.« Translation: Williamson.

No formal scriptural authority

However, God's being bound to the outward word has to be distinguished from a formal scriptural authority. According to Lutheran understanding, Christianity is not a book religion. The object of faith is not the veracity of the Bible, but God's promise in the person of Jesus of Nazareth. The veracity of Scripture has to be measured in accordance with this promise. Thus, Luther states: »And that is the true test by which to judge all books, when we see whether or not they inculcate Christ. [...] Whatever does not teach Christ is not yet apostolic, even though St. Peter or St. Paul does the teaching. Again, whatever preaches Christ would be apostolic, even if Judas, Annas, Pilate, and Herod were doing it.«

Reflected handling of Scripture

This understanding of the scriptural core requires a reflected handling of Scripture. According to Lutheran understanding, the scriptures are not mandatorily interpreted by a magisterium but placed in the responsibility of the individual; each individual must be convinced in his heart that it is true. This expectation, directed at each individual subject, still presents problems in many quarters even today. Insensitive slogans such as »Submission to the Bible text!« merely reveal that people are scared of being responsible for the necessary test of biblical truth by means of their own understanding and thinking. What follows is that one is enjoined to play the Bible out against one's own understanding or thinking. In other words, one is supposed to abandon one's own understanding and thinking in favour of obedience to the biblical word. Or else one succumbs to a (more or less) fervent longing for a definitive interpretation by a higher authority, as may be found in the Roman Catholic Church. However, according to Lutheran understanding, the interpretation of Scripture can neither be delegated to a magisterium of the church nor overcome by obedience that renounces understanding, but commits the individual to apply his or her understanding, thoughts and experience. Scripture does not serve as our standard and guiding principle, because we emphatically assert or even prove its divine origin or infallibility, but only because it reveals itself to the persevering reader as the gospel of the God who gives. Luther's statements about Scripture can only be understood and verified in one way: by picking it up and reading it. According to Lutheran understanding, the Holy Spirit works understanding, not submission to the biblical word whilst refraining from understanding.

The church as »creature of the word«

The core of Lutheran teaching is, as we have seen, God's promise. This central idea also shapes the Lutheran understanding of the church. Church is there, where God's promise is audible. Therefore, according to Lutheran understanding, the church is understood neither collectively as a retrospective union of like-minded people (a kind of religious association) nor legalistically as an outwardly constituted institution for salvation legitimised by an unbroken apostolic succession; instead, it is strictly bound to the proclamation of the gospel in preaching and sacrament. The shortest definition of Luther's understanding of the church is: *Ubi est verbum, ibi est ecclesia* – »Where the word is, there is church«. Everything is contained in the »word« that makes the church what it is. Thus, the Augsburg Confession defines the church in Article VII as »the congregation of saints, in which the Gospel is rightly taught and the Sacraments are rightly administered«. Hence, the preaching of the gospel, baptism and the Lord's Supper are the hallmarks of the church (*notae ecclesiae*).

The Lutheran definition of church has a great ecumenical breadth. It allows all Christian communities to be recognized as churches, in so far as the gospel is preached purely, and the sacraments, baptism and the Lord's Supper are administered in the »right« way – meaning according to Scripture.

No distinction between priests and lay people

The Lutheran understanding of church does not need to make a distinction between lay people and priests. In principle, all Christians are called to the priestly ministry, so that one speaks of the priesthood of all the baptised. In order to prevent the proclamation of the good news from coming to a standstill or becoming inaccessible to people, there is the ministry of public proclamation and sacramental administration. This ministry is also particularly responsible for serving the unity of the church.

4. Freed into the present – life and action in faith

Faith: perception of the present

When taking a look at life and action in faith, we should remind ourselves first of all of the Christian understanding of creation. We have said that »believing in creation« does not mean merely being convinced that the world owes its existence to an unmoved mover or an uncaused cause; it means putting my trust in the world as the living space promised to me and being aware of the present time as given to me. The person who speaks of creation in this way does not understand him- or herself (merely) as one element within a natural context (set in motion by God), but understands the world as a personal promise, and hence, sees the present as a space for action – opened up by God and full of opportunities. How can this trust be understood in more detail?

Sin as mistrust

The best way to cast light onto this trust in the world as life-space promised to me is to examine its opposite, sin, which is a deep-seated mistrust. Sin is first and foremost incapacitating; it means losing trust in the world as the life-space promised to me. So, it also means not being able to experience that acceptance and recognition contained in the promise of life. The thoughts, desires and actions of a person under the power of sin are shaped by this deficit. For the sinner, what should be a bounty becomes a burden. Luther describes the sinner as »curved in on himself« (*homo incurvatus in se ipsum*). This self-centredness is the expression of that deficit, and the different manifestations of sin are to be understood as efforts to compensate for it. People exert pressure on those around them in the hope of hearing that they are good and worthy people. This »curving in on oneself«, revolving around one's own person, is derived from inability to trust in the promise made in creation and to receive its inherent acceptance. This inability makes people themselves responsible for such acceptance, and this responsibility means that they are unceasingly occupied with themselves, seeking their own identity and instrumentalising anyone and anything for the purpose of self-recognition and self-approval.

God's promise as the contradiction of despair

In this way, sin consists in directing the will of humans towards themselves. The sinner's self-centredness is caused by seeking acceptance and recognition. Who am I? Who should I be? Who must I be, if I want to accept myself? How must I change in order to find favour in the eyes of others and therefore in my own eyes? This self-centredness, seeking for an identity that finds favour with others and also with oneself, is contradicted by the gospel. According to Reformation understanding, this contradiction does not consist of a commandment »You shall« (for example: »You shall trust life!«) or »You shall not« (for example, »You shall not revolve around yourself!«). Rather, it offers a gift which interrupts this continuous self-investigation: in the gospel, God promises to accept humans – without prerequisites and unconditionally, so that they can look outside themselves. The trust in this promise of unconditional acceptance liberates a person from ceaseless self-preoccupation and self-contemplation. We are empowered to look outside ourselves and to be self-forgetful in a positive sense.

Perception of the present

Freed from being absorbed with themselves, people are capable of perceiving the present. They are empowered to forget themselves and be completely concentrated, to allow themselves to be determined because they are free from self-care and no longer driven by the question of how they must determine the present. Who am I? Who should I be? Who must I be, if I want to accept myself? How must I change in order to find favour in the eyes of others and therefore in my own eyes? This incessant preoccupation with one's own identity obscures one's view of the present, because then the present can only be seen as something that has to be instrumentalised in order to achieve a higher purpose. In other words, the present cannot be seen as a bounty, but merely as a burden. It becomes an area in which to acquire the right to existence, an area in which I have to make something out of myself.

Detachment from yourself

People revolving around themselves cannot stand back inwardly. Fixing one's gaze on Christ makes one free to find such detachment, because it annuls the questions about securing one's own existence. Then one is able to step back and let oneself be determined with confidence. This is how the theologian Oswald Bayer expresses God's justifying love: »It shines wherever we stand back from ourselves – particularly so, when we can laugh at ourselves. It also shines when we forget ourselves in our work, fully concentrated, or when we are in conversation and listening closely to our partner. And it is also effective when we mercifully manage to fall asleep in spite of glaringly unfinished work – to fall asleep undeservedly, ›without any merit or worthiness in me‹. ›It is in vain that you rise up early and go late to rest‹ – at your desk, for example – ›eating the bread of anxious toil; for he gives sleep to his beloved (Ps 127:2).‹« Looking to Christ, faith gains serenity and freedom: it is granted a kind of liberty which frees it from the desire to instrumentalise the diverse possibilities offered by life in order to secure its existence. In this way, the present can come into unadulterated focus; the freedom that is granted gives rise to detachment and a sense of proportion: the necessary scope for action.

Not aversion from the world, but conversion to the world

Looking to Christ therefore does not mean turning one's back on the world, but rather a new approach to the world, a »conversion to the world«. The saving promise of creation is repeated again in Christ: given to you that you may live! »Conversion to the world« means being able to approach the world quite naturally, as candidly and unspoiled as children. It therefore does not come as a surprise that it was from his children that Luther learned his unconstrained and direct way of believing. Luther recalls strikingly that he once took his little son in his arms and spoke to him as follows: »You are our Lord's little fool; under His grace and forgiveness of sins, not under the law, you have no fear, you are safe and repent of nothing. Whatever you do, it is unspoiled.« This trusting orientation towards the world is founded on confidence in God's gracious acceptance: precisely because you are liberated from the burden of justifying yourself and securing your identity by looking to Christ, you can devote your life to the world in unspoiled naiveté! Precisely because you do not have to be anxious about anything, you can take an unbiased view of the world in all its possibilities. And that means: however you do it, it is unspoiled – freed from the impure desire to regard everything only under the aspect of how it may serve to prove one's own right to exist. Unspoiled, because one's relationship with the world does not attempt to look beyond what is visible.

Sense and taste for the finite

According to Christian understanding, God is not to be found in any special areas of life and not in any mysterious »background worlds« which can only be reached by some particular spiritual practices. On the contrary, according to Christian understanding God is to be found in, with and among everyday things: »Take and eat, this is given for you!« The eternal gift is bestowed in the finite, not beyond the finite. Faith does not long for metaphysical ulterior worlds, or yearn for what is infinite, but looks rather to find meaning and taste for the finite. Thus, according to Lutheran understanding, faith is not about charging up some special areas of life in a religious way, but rather about coping with and assuming responsibility for existence as such. Christ converts us to the world. This explains the Lutherans' high esteem for everyday life. »Belief« does not mean that one considers metaphysical facts to be true; it means a practical conduct of life which makes God divine by trusting God's promise and living one's life according to this trust – a day-to-day life that is more or less exciting, following the laws of nature.

Promised more than we can keep?

While we have tried to understand what it means to live looking at Christ, it remains doubtful whether this has not been exaggerated, made too much of; a high ideal may have been confused with ambivalent reality. »Looking to Christ in life ...« – do we Christians actually do that? Or do we just say that we are doing it? And is it not true that this claim is repeatedly refuted by reality?

It would be totally wrong to speak of the Christian's existence in an exalted fashion. Indeed, faith is liberation to life. But Christians do not always live as those liberated, even though they are. Faith is not a possession, but something that is always threatened by darkness and doubt. Freedom and calm in the face of existence are not something the believer possesses; rather, in regarding the cross, people are liberated from the present more and more and wrenched away from revolving around themselves.

Distinction between belief and believers

The existence of Christians is described in an exalted fashion if one essential distinction is disregarded: that between belief and the believer. We do not live in the light of glory; our lives are by no means determined by faith alone. The believer is »at once righteous and a sinner« (*simul iustus et peccator*). This sentence from the Lutheran Confessions is scandalous; for sin, as we have seen, is unbelief and mistrust. If the believer is said to be always a sinner, that is just another way of saying that he continues to be a non-believer, somebody who does not trust God's promise and is only focused on himself in all respects.

A description of the Christian existence which does not take account of this fact and pretends that the believers are determined by faith alone, will always seem foreign to the believer. That will ultimately either lead the believer to despair or prevent him from admitting his doubt and distrust, forcing him to speak of his own existence in a deceitful and downright repugnant way.

Acceptance remains bound to Christ

Even for Christians, their own life is never something that makes them acceptable to God. We can only find acceptance in Christ, not through our own lives. In Christ we experience God's acceptance, but with regard to ourselves we are (and remain) sceptical. We remain unworthy of God's acceptance. The phrase »at once righteous and a sinner« is a brutal expression of this truth: in our own eyes we will always continue to be people with an entirely self-centred will, who do not trust the promise of life and therefore try to find »security« in themselves. Over and over again, the experience of God's acceptance is drawn into this selfishness and instrumentalised by this self-will. What are we confronted with, if we unsparingly ask what our real motives are? Which desires really determine us, and which mechanisms compel our thinking? Do not we constantly contradict the truth we supposedly believe in whenever we think and act, because our will is evidently not determined by this truth, but rather by our selfishness? By looking to Christ we may find that we are often cut off from this selfishness, and can thus experience freedom. By looking to Christ, not to ourselves!

Trust in the face of mistrust

What does »trust« mean in the face of this mistrust, in the face of being »sinful through and through«? What does it mean, as we have said at the beginning of this chapter, to live by trust in Christ and to have one's identity determined in that way? What is the sense of such statements, given that the believer seeks to determine his own identity in all things? Is it just an empty phrase? If we are cut off from our own selfishness (merely) from time to time, can we speak of a life of Christian practice? When rightly understood, this is indeed justified. Christians are people involved in a movement; they have been »sent on their way«, offered a direction in their lives. It is clear that we cannot abandon Christ, neither in temptation, nor in struggle or doubt. We cannot let go of Christ, even when we discover that our will is determined by that ominous selfishness that denies us access to the present. We do not let go of him, because from Christ we hope to find salvation, we look to him and flee to him in all our selfishness. Faith is not a static mode of existence, but a movement of flight. People who were able to experience liberation to life in the light of the cross have been placed on a certain road. They have been granted access to a place which allows them to break out of their constant self-centredness again and again. Thus they are borne up by the hope of being frequently cut off from their self-interest. They have been given access to the place which may be looked at by those who are only looking for themselves. Faith means trusting in the promise of life given in, with and among everyday things, »Take and eat!« In the face of tensions and failures, of adversities and pain, in the face of plaguing doubt, one constantly forgets this promise of life, but nonetheless this promise is clearly repeated, allowing us to take hold of the present confidently – in the »here and now«, again and again.

What about morality and ethics?

Christian existence – as we have said – is the trusting approach to life. Does this definition of Christian existence not take too little regard for morality? Should we not also discuss the actions to which Christians are obliged – those actions which they regard as obligations for themselves and those which they consider obligatory for others? In recent years, the Church's public statements have mostly been concerned with ethical messages. Apparently, this corresponds to the self-understanding of the mainstream churches, which see themselves as central institutions for determining social values.

What contribution do Christians make to the ethical discourse?

By ethics we mean the reflection on the demands of morality. Very diverse groups are involved in the ethical discourse in society, arguing from very different world views. What contribution do Christians have to offer? Do they know better what morality requires in detail? Or is it so, that Christians do not call attention to moral demands at all?

First of all, Christians will point out what is common to all of us, whether good or evil, socially compatible or not, delinquent or law-abiding, behaving in a morally exemplary way or refusing to do so: every human being is a sinner. When humans are regarded as sinners, the perspective is shifted. What difference does it make for one's perception of others and of oneself, when the human being is seen to be a sinner?

Understanding instead of condemning

The doctrine of sin is a guide to dealing with oneself. Adhering to this tradition means discovering oneself. Make no mistake here: it is about discovering yourself, not others. It is precisely this self-knowledge that leads to a changed perception of others and their actions. Their actions are based on the same basic determination of the will that guides our day-to-day actions. If we have a sense of this tendency in us, then we are also aware that the effects of this tendency and the way it is expressed are certainly important, but that they do not distinguish us qualitatively from other people and their actions, or even make us superior to them. It is rather so that other people's actions confront us with our own being. Other people's misdeeds thus give us the opportunity to ponder on ourselves. They raise our consciousness, so that we sense that other people's misbehaviour is based on the same fears, the same blindness and the same ignorance towards the needs of our fellows that guides our own day-to-day actions. Instead of adopting a judgment mode and dissociating ourselves from the deeds of others as something completely alien to us and therefore »incomprehensible«, we can understand their deeds as something from which we have been fortunately spared: »There but for the grace of God go I.«

Thus, the real dynamism with reference to sin becomes clear: the term »sin« is not used as a guide to moral judgments, but is an attempt to initiate understanding. The term »sin« enables us to understand others (empathically) rather than to disassociate ourselves from them in judgment mode. I am like others, and the others are like me – dependent on God's promise: »Look to Christ, that is how I see you!«

Critical of moral regulations

It is essential for Christians to introduce a second aspect into the ethical discourse: ethical appeals do not enable us to fulfil the demands. »You should« is not the same as »you can«. There is – as Luther put it – »no strength« in the commandment.

Why is that so? The answer is to be found in the core of all moral commandments: love. Love is something that cannot be commanded. I cannot love in order to love; love is based on the being of another person. Love cannot be attained by someone who is only concerned with love itself; for a person who simply has a high regard for love and wants to achieve it will certainly fail to reach the beloved. Love is achieved when I am concerned with the person I love, not when I am interested in love itself. A person who loves does not act on account of love, but out of love. This means that the basic question of an ethic which understands acting out of love as the core of normative-ethical demands cannot be: »What should we do?« because love is not something that can be directly aimed at. Love precedes our desire, because it is not determined by our desire, but determines it. Love cannot be commanded; one must be empowered and freed to love.

What is given to me?

If love cannot be commanded, and one must be freed to love, then the crucial question is: »How are we made capable of love?« or »How are we freed to love?« In response to these questions faith, which is trust in God's promise through the person of Jesus of Nazareth in advance of all human activity, claims to provide an answer. Therefore, the starting point of Christian ethics is not human action, but God's promise. Its fundamental question is not »What should I do?«, but »What is given to me?«

The task of Christian ethics

The task of theological ethics concerns first and foremost understanding. It consists in asking about the consequences of such trust in God's unconditional promise for human action itself. Let us formulate some questions of Christian ethics: when people trust in Christ as the one who vouches for a person's past and future deeds, how does that enable them to find inner peace, since there is no need for them to be responsible for their own salvation? When a human being is freed from instrumentalising the various possibilities of action in order to secure salvation, to what extent is that person given the power to take a liberated view of the space for creative being, so that a sense of distance and proportion joins the freedom thus granted to provide the necessary scope for action?

In what way is the human being, who is freed from looking anxiously into the future by trust in Christ, capable of perceiving the present and all the possibilities and opportunities for action that it offers, so that he can do what is necessary just »here and now«, simply because, in Luther's words, he »is [...] satisfied with what is presently at hand« and does not wish to »be their master and ruler for the future«.

Trust as empowerment to love

We have found that Christian ethics, which speak of faith in God's promise, provides an answer to the question, »How can I become capable of love?«. From our previous reflections, it should be clear that Christian ethics are supposed to explore the extent to which trust in God's promise empowers a person to love. Love is always directed to another subject, insofar as love is interested in the well-being of another subject. The intention of an act of love is to create and nurture the well-being of the beloved subject. Thus, liberation to love means nothing more than to allow the person to direct his or her actions towards the loved one. Christian ethics has to answer the question of how far trust in Christ fulfils the law, that is to say, to what extent people are empowered to direct their actions towards the well-being of others. Here, too, we may formulate some questions of Christian ethics: to what extent does trust in the divine promise lead to the calmness which enables one to venture on the deeds of love? To what extent do the deeds of love depend on that liberated perspective on the creative possibilities of existence which is made possible by trust in Christ? To what extent do the deeds of love require such a perception of the present and of their inherent possibilities and opportunities for action which »is [...] satisfied with what is presently at hand«, so that one recognizes – as did the Good Samaritan – the specific need of the other person as a chance for creative action? All in all, how does faith empower people to an »existence in love«, enabling them to make the well-being of others the motive of their own actions?

Proper action

To be liberated to the present means to be liberated for others whom we encounter in the present with their specific concerns and needs. An ethic of the present is therefore interested in the proper action, in what needs to be done – in the here and now. This does not mean that an ethic of the present does not need to take heed of the future as well. On the contrary, what we do in the present has consequences for the future. That is just why we need a sober view that sees what is required, makes a realistic assessment of the consequences and takes rational decisions. We need an unrestricted view of the world, not an anxious concentration on ourselves. This is precisely what is made possible by faith: people made righteous by God do not have to acquire their own righteousness, constantly observing themselves and their own moral quality. To put it in a nutshell: they do not have to worry about their own morality, but are allowed to see others and their worries and needs. Freed from revolving around themselves and their own moral excellence, they can devote themselves to this with the necessary sobriety. An ethic of the present is not interested in the question of what is »good« and must be realised, but quite soberly in what the situation requires and what needs to be done. Therefore, Christians do not have to be always looking out for special, extraordinary acts. For the believer, according to Luther, »there is no distinction in works. He does the great and the important as gladly as the small and the unimportant, and vice versa.«

What is to be done?

Freed from concern for their own moral quality, Christians do not have to ask »What should I do?« or even more dramatically »What good thing is to be done?«, but just the simple question »What needs to be done?« Christians are not interested in their own moral excellence and do not ask about actions and deeds which give them increased moral status; they want to know how to gain an adequate perception of the present. In order to shape the world, it is necessary to perceive it – in such a way that we can see what really matters. And this perception enables us to see what really matters, because we have an unobstructed view for the present and its challenges which is not blinded by an anxious vision of the future and cramped recollections of the past. Those who have been given a promise of the future have a clear view for the present and its challenges. They can take responsibility because they are free to respond. This is just what lies at the core of Lutheran ethics: those who are liberated from »You shall« can do what ought to be done.

Happiness and morality

When we pay attention to our responsibility for our neighbour, does that not indicate that the Christian life is after all a moral existence, but not a pleasurable one? One is indeed often confronted with the notion that happiness and morality are incompatible with one another. Accordingly, moral behaviour which is – in some way or other – committed to the well-being of others is seen to be the opposite of action in the interests of one's own well-being, intended to lead to one's own happiness. Apparently, one has to make a choice between an existence committed to happiness or one that is committed to morality. This clear distinction between (personal) happiness and morality not only presents us with the question of whether one can be happy without taking liberties against morality, but also with the question of whether one can behave morally without sacrificing one's pursuit of happiness. There appears to be two alternatives: either morality which renounces happiness, or happiness which renounces morality. We can find such conceptions in the Christian tradition as well, for example in the image of the broad and narrow ways. On the broad way all the pleasures of life are to be found, while the narrow way leads to God. But is it really the case that morality and happiness, meaning one's own well-being, are mutually exclusive?

The relationship between happiness and morality

It is not unusual to hear that happiness and morality stand in opposition to one another, but this is in contradiction to a different, albeit mostly unspoken and intuitive maxim on the relationship between one's own well-being and consideration for other people's interests. The philosopher Max Horkheimer has observed that happiness and morality often accompany one another and writes: »Whoever is happy needs no malice.« There seems to be some kind of connection between one's own well-being and the consideration of other people's interests. Even in our everyday dealings with each other we seem, at least intuitively, to assume that such a connection exists. We often excuse bad behaviour by blaming it on a state of dissatisfaction, and vice versa: we have higher expectations of others when they are »in a good mood«. Popular culture is already aware of this, at least with regard to singing as an expression of gaiety and good cheer, for in the words of a well-known German folk song: »Where there is song you can safely stay, wicked people have no songs.«

Love – prerequisite for happiness and morality

Our considerations point in the direction of Horkheimer's thoughts. Being able to stop revolving around oneself is the decisive factor for a life of happiness and satisfaction; it is also the decisive factor for a moral life. Those who manage to break out of this self-centredness will be liberated to love. The person who is liberated to love is capable of serving others. Only those who can meet others in an attitude of goodwill are interested in their worries and needs at all. Interest sets creativity free. That is why Augustine says, »Love and do what you will.« Augustine means to say: when someone loves, their perception and their actions will be shaped by love – in a way that is beneficial to the well-being of their neighbour. An existence which is open to others and one which is happy are two sides of the same coin; being open to others in love makes us richer and happier ourselves.

Christian Lehnert

Descent and Ascent

On Lutheran Worship

1. An exotic metaphor to start with

Sea anemones are molluscs that look like flowers in the sea. At low tide, they shrivel up and lie on the stones like the guts of an animal. But as soon as the tide returns, they blossom, open their delicate tentacles, and breathe the sea water. These creatures are firmly fixed, but nonetheless in motion. They sway with the waves and are soft to the touch. They consist almost entirely of water in the midst of water, yet they have their own shape and colour. They live and grow in the sea.

What brings me to think about these creatures? The forms and feelings of Lutheran worship seem to resemble these beings in many respects. Just as the sea anemones absorb the water, open up and let it flow through them, so too are our services permeated by something external. One might say that they exist in the endless ocean of God. This sea which surrounds them from outside is at one and the same time within them, giving them nourishment and substance. The mystery of God is both within and beyond our prayers and hymns and preaching. The worship liturgy is directed towards the transcendent, seeking and awaiting the God who is coming, who both occurs within it and forms it. Like the soft sea animal with its open mouth, that breathes and drinks the water. And when you see a sea anemone under the waves, don't you have the feeling it is singing?

2. »The former ascends, and the latter descends«

According to Luther's understanding, the church service breathes: the worshippers give something away and they receive something. They bring something to God, in silence and speech and song, in thanksgiving and prayer; but they also listen and experience a change within themselves. They express themselves, as they breathe in God's strange, gracious consolation. As they worship, people look upwards, and they are seen by God. They speak, and they listen. At the consecration of the Castle church in Torgau (1544), Martin Luther described this in classical fashion. He said »that our dear Lord himself may speak to us through his holy Word and we respond to him through prayer and praise«.[4]

And elsewhere Luther writes of this movement to and fro: »We must, therefore, not confound these two – the mass and the prayers, the sacrament and the work, the testament and the sacrifice. For the one comes from God to us, through the ministration of the priest, and demands our faith, the other proceeds from our faith to God, through the priest, and demands His answer. The former descends, the latter ascends …«[5]

Descent and ascent. We receive, and we act. We are spoken to, and we answer. These things must not be confused – but the two aspects tend to merge in the breath of the liturgy, permeating one another and thus becoming recognisable. For we en-

---

4 LW 51,333 (»daß unser lieber Herr selbst mit uns rede durch sein heiliges Wort, und wir wiederum mit ihm reden durch Gebet und Lobgesang.« WA 49,588).

5 Translation at www.lutherdansk.dk/web-babylonian%20captivitate/martin%20luther.htm.

counter the »holy word«, it »descends«, and in it God speaks. But this experience of the »holy word« only becomes real and true for us in faith. Our faith answers, expresses itself, and bears witness to an inner change that far transcends our understanding and perception.

This inseparable intermingling of address and response is important and may not be unravelled on one side or the other. On the one hand, there is no place during worship, neither in a particular ritual nor in a text, where we can, as it were, grasp God, where he can be objectively comprehended. No, he always remains inaccessible. Worship is dependent on his strange closeness. That is experienced by faith. On the other hand, worship is not merely a lecture or a performance made by humans. It is also not a purely symbolic mediation of something external to such presentations, for example, of a certain world-view. It is not a pious dialogue, and it is not a lecture. It is also not a technique for perceiving God. No, the service pulsates and breathes. It resembles the sea anemones, for whom the water is both their external environment and their inner substance. That is God's nature: infinitely greater than all human activity in worship, and taking place in its centre. He remains alien to us, yet he comes closer to us than we are to ourselves.

3. The form of the Mass

This »descent and ascent«, the liturgical intermingling of address and response, is particularly evident in a liturgical form that shaped Lutheranism like no other – the Mass. Lutherans developed it out of the tradition of the medieval Latin Mass, which dated back many centuries. They preserved essential elements and made corrections to problematic developments, especially to misleading formulations concerning the Lord's Supper. Luther took over, translated and revised the form of the Mass in his liturgical orders of 1523 (*Formula Missae et Communionis*) and 1526 (»German Mass and Order of worship«). The form of Mass is characterized by a constant change of perspective and a spiral of ups and downs. Let us examine some of the important stages in order to gauge the depths of our divine service.

4. The opening

In accordance with the Evangelical Service Book, the service begins with an Invocation, that is to say a solemn declaration: »In the name of the Father and the Son and the Holy Spirit.« The minister speaks these words to the congregation. It is not we who begin the service, not by our own actions. We act in representation of the Triune God, under his power and blessing.

Certainly, it is obviously a human being who is speaking – the minister. But these words do not have a meaning that could come from a human. We can only hear them and receive them. They name the intangible origin of all that we can do. God defines this origin. It is not we who have the first word.[6] These words are what make us into a community of believers.

---

6 This is not so clear if the service begins with the words »We are holding this service in the name of the Father and the Son and the Holy Spirit.«

What a special and salutary moment, when that name is mentioned, which goes before all else! Strictly speaking, this is not the uttering of a name, but testimony to a revelation. These few words tell an intimate story about God and how he reveals himself to us – as father and creator, permeating all things; as Jesus Christ, who died on the cross and rose again; and as spirit, bringing people together in this threefold name.

Significantly, the invocation repeats the baptismal formula »I baptise you in the name of the Father and the Son and the Holy Spirit.« The recollection of the beginning of every relationship to God, which does not take place at our own initiative but is granted to us, is brought back to mind at the beginning of the service.

»The former descends, the latter ascends.« Listening and speaking come together at the very start of the service. The invocation is followed by a dialogue. The minister speaks to the congregation: »The Lord be with you!« And the congregation responds with a reciprocal greeting: »And with your spirit.« Minister and congregation enter into a relationship, they take on roles – exactly in that space that God grants us by his proximity.

At the beginning of the service everything is open. The first words show that something is taking place here which goes far beyond the person who is self-determined and autonomous. What is essential lies ahead of us.

5. *Kyrie eleison*

»*Kyrie eleison*. Lord, have mercy.« This first chant at the Mass is a fervent and direct appeal for mercy. When the Godhead comes close, humans are in danger. Their existence is helpless, divested of language and deprived of their own self, as soon as even a wisp of God's presence comes into contact with human reality: »Woe is me! I am lost, for I am a man of unclean lips, and I live among a people of unclean lips; yet my eyes have seen the King, the Lord of hosts!« (Isaiah 6:5) This is the Bible's account of the words of the prophet Isaiah as he saw a vision of worship in heaven. The proximity of God immediately made him acutely aware of his own state: his broken existence and entanglement in guilt. The first reaction, a primal religious reflex when confronted by the presence of Almighty God, is the appeal for mercy – and that is also so in our services.

The *Kyrie* originates in pre-Christian cultic greetings of the rising sun. Once they sung »Helios, have mercy on us!« in reverence of the God Sol when he rose up and brought the day. The Roman emperors elevated sun worship to the imperial cult. Whenever the Sun Emperor, the divine ruler and *Kyrios*, entered a city, the loyal or enslaved masses at the wayside sang these words in Greek: »*Kyrie, eleison*. Lord, have mercy!«

What could be more natural for the early Christians than to use these very words when welcoming their *Kyrios*, the Christ, as the true and liberating light? They added: »*Christe eleison*. Christ, have mercy.« They professed Christ as the coming and everlasting Lord, as the true sun on the horizon of the empire.

Ever since those early days of Christian worship, the *Kyrie* has been spoken or sung in churches as a request for forgiveness and in praise of Christ present. He is our true and only

Lord. In his light the form of our life is revealed, uncovered and bare, and his coming outshines everything when he consoles and heals.

6. Glory to God in the highest

»Glory to God in the highest,« sings the minister, and the congregation: »And on earth peace to people of good will.« The words of the second canticle in the Mass, *Gloria in excelsis Deo*, point in two opposing directions. Seated in the pews, we hear the angels, powers from on high. In the Christmas story, Luke the Evangelist tells how shepherds in the field first heard these words in the night when Jesus was born: »And suddenly there was with the angel a multitude of the heavenly host praising God and saying, ›Glory to God in the highest heaven, and on earth peace among those whom he favours!‹« (Luke 2:13–14) Biblical images of other spheres are opened up above us as a gathering of worshippers. With this song we become witnesses of a worship service in another world. We harken.

That is the one direction: the song descends …

But the Gloria is also an intense prayer call. We praise the God who wants to bring us peace, Shalom. We accompany the heavenly chorus with our human voices. Prayerfully, we join in the singing, and our hymn rises.

Between the worlds, the music resounds. Human and angelic voices sing in unison. This hymnus [which is sung by many congregations at high festivals as the Greater Doxology] originates from the eastern part of the Roman Empire, where it was sung by Greek-speaking Christians in the early morning, at sunrise. It belongs to daybreak, to the dwindling darkness at the end of the night, when first contours and colours appear and the dew falls – a song to celebrate the emergence of God's new world.

In the Latin West, these verses first appeared in the Christmas mass. From there, the song also made its way into the weekly church services and has thus been handed down to us. Until the twelfth century, ordinary priests were not allowed to sing the Gloria – it was reserved for bishops. Presumably its status was unclear, too confusing and dangerous – these mysterious transitions and harmonies between the tongues of humans and angels.

7. The Collect of the Day

»Let us pray!« With these words the minister now appeals to the congregation and speaks or chants a prayer to the altar. This prayer during the opening part of the service is called the Collect of the Day. The name is derived from the Latin verb *colligere*, meaning to collect or to gather together. The idea is to gather all the personal prayer topics, the various emotions and expectations, doubts, hopes and questions that move each individual. In this way the fellowship of believers is formed.

The prayer of the day changes each week and also at festival seasons and it has a particular structure. It is short, and one may say that it reproduces in a concise form the basic structure of all Christian prayer, as a sort of »short prayer grammar«. This happens in four stages:

1) The first step is already an adventure. God is named and spoken to directly. When Moses was a shepherd in the

desert, God appeared to him in the burning bush. When asked about his name, he replied, »I am who I am.« That means that he refused to give his name. God remains nameless. He comes again and again, unexpectedly, unforeseen, and mysteriously – as the one who is and will be. No word, no image can express his being. But we need to direct our prayers, so we use linguistic images as a form of address. We speak to him with the familiar »Thou«. But these linguistic images have a special characteristic: they are not able to define God and do not intend to do so, but they are searching for him. In all our prayer formulas, we are aware that God cannot in fact be named. Those who pray express their changing relationship to God in open images. The forms of address are mostly taken from the Bible, especially from the psalms. God is called »father« and »creator«; he is described as »kind«, »eternal«, »loving« or »triune« God.

2) Secure in having made contact with God, the prayers of the day now make allowance for recollection. We look back at the basis and justification for all prayer and ascertain that God has shown himself in the past. In prayer, we recall what has gone before. In many cases the prayer recounts a biblical story in a few words or recalls experiences that people have made with God. At the same time, it refers to the most important topics of the readings, especially of the Sunday Gospel. The tone of this recollection is thanksgiving and praise. For every prayer to God is sustained by the certainty that God spoke first to us »through his holy Word, and we in turn speak to him through prayer and praise«. »The former descends, and the latter ascends.«

3) So, the third step comes next: a sudden change to intercession. If God was »the one who he was«, then may he be so

again, here and now. Christians ask that the transforming power that is in God's presence may come into their lives. The worshippers, who had just been recognising the traces of God's action in the world, now ask that these traces become opportunities for new encounters with God. They pray for support and aid, for faith and hope, for vigour and healing.

It is striking how suddenly prayer requests enter the room of memories. As we look back, our gaze abruptly turns ahead towards the unfulfilled and inaccessible action of God.

Prayer itself actually takes place in the gap between these two impulses. God was there, as we recall; may he return, that is what we hope and pray. He has left traces in real life, like tracks in the snow, witnessing to him who has been there, but is now absent for us. Thus we pray in the same breath for his presence, sensing and hoping for God's nearness. Prayer becomes tangible in this gap – it is experienced as a trace and a place. In this sense, it is a placeholder in expectation of the inaccessible God who is absent, yet present.

4) The prayer finally unfolds and radiates in the doxology. God, who embraces eternity, is here. He becomes real in the prayer itself. This doxology is often a standard formula, not because someone had run out of ideas, but because for those who pray the words fail. They can seek support in set phrases. The formulas include language from olden times, figures of speech tested by time which give assurance and lift the worshippers beyond what they could express in their own words and thoughts. It is not only the congregation here that speaks, but also all those who have gone before and will later follow in the great invisible Church of God.

The closing words of the prayer are well-known and indicate to the congregation that they may respond jointly with »Amen«, confirming and adopting what has been said. This prayer is spoken by all, collectively – the Collect of the Day.

8. The readings

We clearly hear God's »holy word«, as Luther called it, in the readings. As it is read out to us, we are silent. We are reminded of our origins and hear how God revealed himself. The readings consist of excerpts from the Bible (so-called pericopes), from the Old and New Testaments. The selection is in parts very old. The texts are related to each other and convey the special meaning of each Sunday or feast day. Very often the Gospel text is in the foreground – which is why it should in every case be read.

The Bible reading usually takes place at a raised lectern. In this way the readings are quite literally lifted out of the many areas in which we modern humans are closely surrounded by the spoken word. Here we find a special language, words and phrases in which God himself happens and works. The texts are framed by various canticles and chants – for example by the Hallelujah. They also serve to underline the significance of the readings.

But let us take a closer look at what it means when we say that God's word is happening here. At first glance, Holy Scripture has a melancholy role to play in the Protestant church service: it stands for the past. The Bible looks back and tells of what took place. Writing replaces the close fellowship with God that was experienced in the history of Israel and during

Christ's time on earth. In place of Jesus' voice, eyes and healing hands, we simply have a book.

However, this historical aspect is only superficial. Luke's Gospel tells how a reading took place at a service which was also Jesus' first public appearance in Nazareth (Luke 4:14–29). Jesus, as a young man of religious maturity, is called to read from the scroll of the prophets in the synagogue. He reads a passage from the book of Isaiah, an eschatological prophecy. He reads about hope – about blind people »whose eyes are opened«, about prisoners who are »to be released« and about »the year of the Lord's favour«. Luke only records one cryptic sentence out of Jesus' interpretation of these words: »Today this scripture has been fulfilled in your hearing.« These words are drowned in the ensuing turmoil. One sentence, starting with the word »today«, and the levels fall apart like an imploding television set. Jesus crashes into the context of the prophecy like a meteor. The moment in which he reads the text becomes the moment in which it becomes real: »Today this scripture has been fulfilled in your hearing.«

In the blink of an eye, Jesus, as the Son of God and Messiah, reveals from Scripture how he understands his role. Only Jewish tradition can make it clear who he really is: the Christ and Lord at the end of time. At the same time, he himself enters into Scripture. Jesus becomes part of an ongoing narrative, a Gospel. He is practically incorporated into the written language, transformed into text and type, recitation and transcription, exegesis and preaching, Bible and canon. Later he will be printed and digitized, translated and published. So one can say: a reading from Scripture, reported in Scripture, makes God recognisable and real as Scripture. A book, the Bible, shows us how God speaks to us through all things and in all things, as Creator, Logos, and as the Spirit that permeates everything.

That is why Holy Scripture is so central to Protestant Christians in worship. It makes all that we do in our worship service comprehensible; it is God's message which changes us and transforms us, so that we can respond to it. Protestant worship derives its meaning and form by reference to the Word. As Luther put it: »And this is the sum of the matter: Let everything be done so that the Word may have free course instead of the prattling and rattling that has been the rule up to now. We can spare everything except the Word. Again, we profit by nothing as much as by the Word.«[7]

It is surprising that the biblical readings, which lie at the heart of Protestant worship culture, are nowadays by no means uncontroversial. It shows how quickly the scales tilt and how difficult it is »not to confound these two: ... the former descends, the latter ascends ...« Critics of the biblical readings repeatedly lead their attacks while waving the banner of »comprehensibility«. Is it reasonable to confront modern readers with these complicated and confusing texts dating from late antiquity? Who can make anything of them? How can you still reach people with that?

»The former descends, and the latter ascends.« The origin of worship is the experience of strangeness. What »descends«

---

7 LW 53,14 (»Aber die Summa sei die, daß es ja alles geschehe, daß das Wort im Schwange gehe ... Es ist alles besser nachgelassen, denn das Wort. Und es ist nichts besser getrieben, denn das Wort.« Martin Luther, Von Ordenung Gottisdiensts, Kirche und Schule, Schriften III, edited by Albrecht Beutel, Verlag der Weltreligionen, Berlin 2015, p. 54).

goes beyond human imagination. Whatever a person says about it, whatever the response in prayers and thoughts, it points to what is inexpressible. God, who is exceedingly greater than I, can only approach me as a stranger. Otherwise he would not be God, but merely an image of him that I have formed. Even before he showed himself, I would want to have categorised him, in an ideology or a scientific knowledge base. Anyone who expects comprehensibility in a service of worship is asking for something which is self-contradictory. God can never become comprehensible.

But that which »ascends« is also valid. Purely incomprehensible and unapproachable rites and words would contradict what constitutes a service as it is understood by Protestants: contact. God and people come close to one another. I need to understand in order to have an experience. In this sense, a service needs to be understandable. We find a new recognition of ourselves and our lives in it and in the light of God. We pray that God may be close to us, and that always means a deeper understanding of his ways with us.

We are walking a tightrope here and are in danger of falling off on one side or the other. The strangeness and mystery of God is supposed to find resonance within us, without losing this strangeness. Consolation and admonition, hope, healing and transformation – all these are offered and promised to us. They are not in our possession. Biblical readings always require fresh exegesis and interpretations which resound for all the hearers.

In this context, it is no coincidence that liturgical song and music were always characteristic for Lutheran worship. In singing, language is strengthened and intensified in its effect. At the same time, music transcends words and lifts them to spheres that elude verbal expression. Christians sing biblical verses and prayers because they receive and express more in these words than just information and statements. They are touched and want to absorb them into their being. They sense the breath of God. They are made Christians in the biblical language, celebrating the grace of an unceasing creation from the Word.

Readings are the wings of Christian piety. Just as birds of passage keep up a constant rhythm during their flight, never ceasing, beating their wings against the air resistance, and thus passing over oceans and continents, so Christians persevere in their readings for centuries. The order of the readings in our churches, this fixed sequence of texts Sunday by Sunday, is equivalent to a pulse which lasts for years, beating unbelievably slowly, yet steadily. Texts are repeated, forming a kind of dream language and a deep memory for Christian communities since their very beginnings.

9. The creed spoken together

The creeds are shared by Christians across time and space and denominational boundaries. During worship services it is usually either the so-called Apostles' Creed (first mentioned around 390) or the Niceno-Constantinopolitan Creed (adopted at a Council in 451) which is spoken. The phrases which have been handed down over generations, recited in unison, give reality to a fellowship which is far more than we know.

Speaking the Creed in chorus during a church service can be understood in three ways: 1) It is our response to God's Word, heard in the readings and the sermon. 2) We listen as we recite our basic beliefs in images – that is to say, we are seeking traces of God's action as we speak these words. 3) It is joint prayer for a living faith.

What does it actually mean to say »I believe«? I often say this in everyday life, when I am not entirely sure about something: »I believe it's going to be warm today,« and then later in the afternoon I lie in the grass in the sunshine, dozing contentedly to the sound of the flies and bumblebees, and my belief has become certainty.

This is obviously not what is meant when I recite the Creed in church with all the others. It is not just speculation. On the contrary: it is the ultimate certainties which are spoken here aloud, even if they are only subjectively perceived as such. In this case »I believe …« is the expression of a deep and unconditional trust, an orientation for life which touches the depths of the soul. Here belief means complete reliance on something. (Such points of reference are presumably to be found in every life, and even those who claim to believe in nothing refer at some point to some basic certainties and values that have no objective justification – but they choose various ones without precisely recognising what they are doing.)

But the words »I believe« do not stand alone. In a Christian church service they are followed by statements, connecting me by content with all who share this confession. They set me apart from those who refuse them or regard them as irrelevant. As a Christian, I confess what I believe: something that can be defined … But then I look around me in the church. All the others are joining in, some of them quietly and unobtrusively, others loudly and utterly convinced, and I get the impression that hardly anyone here means the same thing. I also see how my eight-year-old daughter repeats the words. What does she understand by an »only begotten Son«? And where can that be: »the right hand of God the Father«? Not to mention the gloomy descent »to the dead«.

So it cannot be the content of the words which is decisive. When I say »I believe …«, that goes deeper than I can follow, deeper than the understanding of any of the phrases in the text. »I believe …« – that means that I entrust myself to a mystery, a force that carries me away. As in a maelstrom, the series of sentences whirls me around and sweeps me into the unpredictable and unknown, closer and closer towards a God who cannot even vaguely be grasped in words and figures of speech. My confession is lacking in every case, falling far short of what really happens.

The early Christians tried to summarise the essence of their beliefs in clear and concise phrases which helped them to identify swiftly those who belonged to their faith and to distinguish themselves reliably from outsiders. These confessions played an especially prominent role at baptisms. They defined the new area of life which the baptismal candidate was entering. These ancient confessions are still spoken today by Christians in their church services. When I confess my faith in these words, I am therefore connected spiritually with all those who for almost 2,000 years have understood themselves to belong to the »holy Christian church«, as it says in this Creed, and who are now close to me, concealed within these words. I plunge into a river that runs through the ages, flowing down towards a world to come. One may say that, as I speak these words, I am not expressing something, but rather that »something« is coming towards me – God, the Nameless One, who manifests himself historically in his church. He is realised and takes place in faith, and my response consists only superficially of words or persuasions. In truth, my response involves the whole of my life and all aspects of my existence and actions in this world.

When I say »I believe …«, I am balancing on a tightrope. I can neither reduce the Creed to its contents, nor can I release it from them. A faith that only consisted of knowledge about faith would be nothing more than one world-view among others. But a faith that considers it possible to express everything individually, freely and subjectively drifts away into purely arbitrary feelings, clothing me in my own lonely expectations of transcendence, as if I were standing in front of a mirror. Those are two ways to miss the point of the Credo. That is why the most decisive word of the Creed may well be the concluding »Amen«. Luther translated the Hebrew word as »Of this I am sure.«[8] In other words: I want to believe that. I want to accept what I am saying and hearing, even if I cannot believe it. The »Amen« forms the complete concentration of a religious existence. It represents a leap into the unknown, despite all appearances – a leap into a darkness which it firmly believes to be the one and only true salvation.

10. Intercessions and collections

It is probably the most abrupt interruption of the liturgical flow during a church service: the collection. Suddenly, between the prayers and hymns, people begin to do perfectly

---

[8] Martin Luther, Kleiner Katechismus, Reformation der Frömmigkeit und Bibelauslegung, Schriften II, hrsg. von Thomas Kaufmann, Verlag der Weltreligionen, Berlin 2014, p. 202.

mundane things, rummaging in their wallets and purses for coins or banknotes, doing sums in their heads and pondering on the worthiness of good causes. That is particularly problematic in an age that has raised economic thinking to the leading cultural authority and tends to translate everything into terms of monetary value. Hardly any area of life is in a position to avoid this all-embracing approach. That means that the collection of money in church can easily be misunderstood: is it necessary to pay money for the opportunity of an encounter with God, for the rituals touching upon the divine mystery?

During church services, Christian congregations collect donations in cash or in kind for two reasons:

1) Caring for the needy is a task for all believers who follow Jesus. Service to one's neighbour takes place in expectation of the coming transformation of the world in Christ. Thus, it must logically be ritually visible at our liturgical celebrations. Collecting money is an expression of the fact that faith is always also *diakonia*, the loving and active devotion to fellow human beings.
2) Money was very early seen as a symbol of the gifts brought to the Lord's Table at Holy Communion. It represented the goods of the world which Christians laid on the altar as thanksgiving and sacrifice. In the earliest congregations bread and wine, milk and honey, cheese and olives were collected during worship and later, after the celebration of the Lord's Supper, distributed to the absent needy. When Christianity became the state religion in the Roman Empire and the congregations grew larger, money was collected instead of natural products for purely practical reasons. The Lord's

Supper and the support of the needy were always felt to be two sides of one coin.

In the early centuries of the Christian era, the liturgy of the Lord's Supper began with the General Intercessions, exactly at the conclusion of the liturgy of the Word and before the celebration of the Eucharist. This »Prayer of the Faithful« was the great universal prayer of the Christian Church, and is upheld in the Lutheran churches to this day. The preparation of the gifts, the collection of money and the intercessions are directly related to one another. The participation in the gift of the body and blood of Christ, service to one's neighbour, action and prayer belong together liturgically. For Christian faith is never just a private affair, but shows its inner strength in dealing with the questions and needs of the world. In an increasingly segmented society, which confuses ideological indifference with tolerance, this connection has become important: Christian faith is never confined to itself. It is always realised in the relationship to fellow human beings and to all creation.

11. Holy Communion

For Luther and the Reformers in Wittenberg the Latin Mass was the natural starting point for their reflections on worship. It had developed as a cultic drama, deeply rooted in the area of classical antiquity where cult and theatre were closely connected. The polyphony, the internal tensions and the basic scenic constellation of a chorus and one performer who steps out of the crowd, talks and sings – this all demonstrates the relationship to ancient tragedy. The service of worship was repeatedly described as play, pure and happy like children's play – only here the first and last things are played out, for God is present in all that happens.[9]

The Mass in the narrower sense, the celebration of the Lord's Supper, fulfils Luther's understanding of worship particularly strongly: »The former descends, the latter ascends.« »We must, therefore, not confound these two – the mass and the prayers […]. For the one comes from God to us, through the ministration of the priest, and demands our faith, the other proceeds from our faith to God, through the priest, and demands His answer.« God becomes real in bread and wine, he descends to us. In the same way, however, the Lord's Supper is a symbolic act by the worshippers, a kind of holistic prayer, active preaching and experienced fellowship. Divine and human action are here interwoven like a fine piece of venerable and hard-wearing cloth. In the sacrament there are no more distinctions between inside and outside, action and experience, God and me. Such differentiation can no longer describe what happens.

9 »That is something wonderful which happens in the liturgy: art and reality are united as we become supernatural children in the presence of God … To play a game before God – not to create a work of art, but to be one, that is the innermost essence of the liturgy.« Taken from Romano Guardini, Vom Geist der Liturgie, Herder & Co. GmbH Verlagsbuchhandlung, Freiburg 1922, p. 67.

The preparation takes place at the beginning of the sacramental liturgy, whereby the roles are confusingly assigned. One single person, the minister, goes forward out of the congregation, raises his or her voice and chants or speaks to the others from before the altar: »The Lord be with you.« This greeting is then received and taken up by the chorus, the congregation, and returned in the ancient style: »And with your spirit.« All the interpersonal energy arising in this brief dialogue, all the tension between attachment and detachment, between a sense of communion and a feeling of autonomy, is immediately diverted, as if by a reverse lightning rod, and converted into transcendence, like a jagged flash of light in the sky: »Lift up your hearts!« »We lift them up to the Lord.«

And now the minister chants a prayer, in which the subject of the text grows and expands wider and wider, like waves on the surface of a calm lake, so that the starting point is soon forgotten: »It is indeed meet, right, and salutary that we should at all times and in all places give thanks to You, holy Lord, almighty Father, everlasting God, through Jesus Christ our Lord. You have sent him for the salvation of the world. By his death we have forgiveness of sin and by his resurrection life eternal ...« Who is speaking here? First of all, the minister joins in the others in using »we« and »us«. But this »we« is not identical with those who are present, or even with any specific number of people. It subtly moves up into a higher level, for the minister continues, »In communion with angels and archangels, and with all who served you on earth and worship you now in heaven, we raise our voice to proclaim your glory, for ever praising you and saying: ...« We are no longer just the congregation in church, praying with the pastor. The angels and the heavenly hosts and powers join in the praise. No one speaks here in the first person anymore, there is no I or we. The voices break into celestial song, the music of another world. Here all boundaries fall away; individual identity is lost in a different entity, merging with all believers in one invisible church, the body of Christ. The singers feel the same as the author of the old »Theologia deutsch«, which Luther so valued: »Behold! I, poor fool that I was, imagined it was I, but behold! it [sic] is, and was, of a truth, God!«[10] And so everyone joins in one ancient hymn of praise, the *Sanctus*: »Holy, holy, holy is the Lord of hosts, all the lands are full of his glory.«[11]

---

10 Theologia Germanica. Which setteth forth many fair lineaments of divine truth, and saith very lofty and lovely things touching a perfect life. Trans. by Susanna Winkworth, W.F. Draper, Andover / Boston 1860, p. 14 (»Sieh, ich armer Tor, ich meinte, ich wäre es: nun ist und war es wahrlich Gott.« Theologia Deutsch, nach dem Pfeifferschen Text in neues Deutsch gebracht von Rudolf Alexander Schröder, C. Bertelsmann Verlag, Gütersloh 1948, p. 35).

11 The biblical Greek text: *Hagios, hagios, hagios kyrios Sabaōth. Plērēs pasa hē gēs doxēs autou* (Isaiah 6:3 LXX) was slightly changed in the Latin version of the Missale Romanum (and in Greek liturgies): *Sanctus, Sanctus, Sanctus Dominus Deus Sabaoth. Pleni sunt caeli et terra Gloria tua.* Now one said »Dominus Deus«, and the heavens (caeli) were added to the Earth. The earliest German translation is closer to the original biblical text: Heilig, heilig, heilig ist Gott der Herre Zebaoth. Alle Lande sind seiner Ehre voll.

This song is the first climax of the Communion liturgy. The verses chanted come from the report of a vision dating back thousands of years: »In the year that King Uzziah died, I saw the Lord sitting on a throne, high and lofty; and the hem of his robe filled the temple. / Seraphs were in attendance above him; each had six wings: with two they covered their faces, and with two they covered their feet, and with two they flew. / And one called to another and said: ›Holy, holy, holy is the Lord of hosts; the whole earth is full of his glory.‹ The pivots on the thresholds shook at the voices of those who called, and the house filled with smoke.« With these words from Isaiah 6:1–4 the early prophet tells of his calling, which took place in the year 740 BC when King Uzziah died in Jerusalem.

Isaiah was a »seer« ... but what did he see? Was it something visible, an event, something that he saw and experienced and described? Or could it be the other way round – that this incredible experience actually gained shape in the text itself as the narrator attempted to understand the incomprehensible? Is it valid to speak here at all of something that was »seen«?

The background to this vision of revelation was the worship cult with which Isaiah was familiar in Jerusalem. The readers would envision the Temple of Jerusalem in their mind's eye. To be precise, they would picture the great nave of the sanctuary, that long sacred space containing the sacrificial altar, leading towards the Holy of Holies. Here Isaiah saw God »sitting on a high and lofty throne«, a blatantly simple image indicating more than could be imagined or seen, so that one wonders what Isaiah actually saw. Presumably, it was nothing that was really visible. If it was anything, then a blinding glare, leading to a painful loss of sight, and in his blindness he tried to understand, making use of the images he could call on: the Temple, the nave, the gleaming polished walls. … They denoted what was unthinkable.

The seraphs formed two choirs. They covered their legs and blocked out sight and sound by hiding their eyes and ears as they sang: »Holy, holy, holy is the Lord of hosts; the whole earth is full of his glory.«

»Then one of the seraphs flew to me, holding a live coal that had been taken from the altar with a pair of tongs. / The seraph touched my mouth with it … / Then I heard the voice of the Lord saying, ›Whom shall I send, and who will go for us?‹ And I said, ›Here am I; send me!‹« (Isaiah 6:6–8) Smoke in the temple, smoke from the animal sacrifices, dense smoke coming from scorched meat, and Isaiah's mouth is cauterised. Did the prophet experience this revelation as a kind of excruciating pain which brought his physical existence to piercing implosion?

The experience of God's real presence cannot be expressed in human words. Proximity to God has nothing to do with sight or sound. Isaiah is in the literal sense burnt out, deprived of his speech and his senses. Before Isaiah can say »Here am I,« he is snuffed out. It is no longer »I« who speaks. It is a metamorphosis comparable to that of Saul, whose person was also extinguished and who later said, as Paul: »It is no longer I who lives, but it is Christ who lives in me.« (Galatians 2:20)

The song of the seraphs is very ancient liturgical material. Jewish worship services took it over from the temple cult, and it was then sung by Christians at their very first gatherings. There is hardly any sequence of words in human history that has been so continuously sung in cultic usage. The Sanctus represents a severe liturgical imposition. The congregation sings in a state of extinction. As they sing, they burn inwardly, and coals of fire are put in their mouths. The ashes of their souls lie in the pews. But all this fear, this awe in the presence of God, is overcome by a powerful consolation, a saving echo – a metamorphosis to life. God asks, »Whom shall I send?« And with Isaiah we answer, »Here am I, send me!«

This profound verbal event defines the space in which the sacrament of the altar can take place and be experienced in faith. The liturgy of Holy Communion is a grand sequence of prayers, extending from the Sanctus, the Lord's Prayer and the words of institution to the *Agnus Dei*, »Lamb of God«.

The words of institution

»The former descends, the latter ascends …« In the Early Church, the words of institution of the Lord's Supper were explicitly included in a prayer of comprehensive thanksgiving – giving thanks for our creation and existence, for faith and revelation and for the coming of Jesus Christ into the world.[12] The words of institution were part of a narrative of Christ's works of salvation, so that they served as an element of remembrance in the prayer. Just as abruptly as in the collect of the day, a prayer request follows: the invocation of the Holy Spirit. May this most profound proximity of God and humanity be realised

---

12 The oldest known prayer of this kind is to be found in the »Apostolic Tradition« (*Traditio apostolica*), which is attributed to the presbyter und rival pope Hippolytus of Rome, who died around 235 AD. See Karl-Heinrich Bieritz, Liturgik, Walter de Gruyter, New York / Berlin 2004, p. 316 f.

once again in the Spirit, as it was at the Last Supper of Jesus. May Christ now say, »This is my body,« and »This is my blood.« Here and now, as we celebrate the Lord's Supper! Experienced in the Spirit and in faith, at this very moment!

Lutheran understanding has preserved the character of this prayer in the words of institution at the Lord's Supper. The real presence of God in bread and wine is experienced by the believers through prayer. To be sure, Luther himself felt that the words of institution belonged to the biblical proclamation, for he chanted them to the melody of a Gospel reading. But what is the point of such nuances here? What takes place here is of a comprehensive nature. Everything occurs at the same time and in all places when God happens. Christians are transformed, healed, comforted and welcomed into the body of the risen God. They pray and receive, they seek God and are found by him.

The Agnus Dei

The *Agnus Dei*, which concludes the liturgy of the Lord's Supper, originally belonged to the rite of breaking of bread. Dividing a loaf of bread was already an integral part of Jewish meal rites. The one bread was cut up at the beginning of a meal shared by many. In connection with Jesus' words, who shared such meals with his disciples, the last time on Holy Thursday, this »breaking of bread« had a sharper ring to it: »This is my body.« A body broken and despised.

Home-baked bread in Rome – in the first Christian centuries, large bread rings were brought to the altar in linen bags, where they were crushed by the bishop and the elders. A momentous, symbolic process, which initially took place in silence. One may well imagine the sound: the crumbling noises, the lumps of bread cracking and snapping inside the linen shrouds – a gruesome spectacle: »This is my body.«

When the Western churches began to use unleavened bread, later even small, specially baked wafers known as hosts, this hymn became obsolete, for there was no more breaking of bread in the liturgy. The *Agnus Dei* was shortened to a threefold repetition, sung during the ritual greeting of peace before the Lord's Supper. The believers embraced and kissed each other; and accordingly, at some point in the tenth century, a prayer for peace was added: »Dona nobis pacem, give us peace.« In peace, and transformed into the fellowship of the world to come, we eat of the one bread and drink out of the one cup, as one communion in God.

12. The river and the banks: the sermon

What can we say about the sermon? On our pathway through the worship service we have focussed on certain liturgical elements and passed over others, including the sermon so far. On the one hand, the sermon is closely entwined with the liturgical flow, and its effect depends strongly on the way in which it corresponds to the situation and mood of the service. On the other hand, the sermon belongs to a category of its own, which has to stand out from the rest and to speak for itself, regardless of references to other parts of the service. In the nineteenth century, when the form of Lutheran worship was being reconsidered in all parts of Germany with particular emphasis on the recollection of sources and traditions, Wilhelm Löhe used the following imagery to describe what happens during the liturgy:

»I would like to compare the train of thought in the liturgy of the main church service with a twin-peaked mountain … The first summit is the sermon, and the second is the sacrament of the altar, without which I cannot imagine any service on earth to be complete.«[13]

The way in which encounters with God are imparted differ considerably at these two respective summits. At the Lord's Supper, the participants abandon themselves to liturgical formulas and gestures that altogether transcend thought and reflection. It is as though they were being carried along by a river bearing them beyond their boundaries in the direction of God. In the sermon, by contrast, the resonance occurs precisely on the basis of thought and understanding, as the listeners follow the minister's explanations, now acting as an academic theologian with personal opinions and background. As they listen to the sermon, the believers now feel as though they were on the banks of the river, looking down at it. They reflect critically on their own views, think about their faith and Christian life, and receive consolation or criticism.

By this two-fold mode of action, Protestant worship reveals a certain peculiarity. It is intended to draw people outside themselves into the realm of the divine. To this purpose, it strives to produce moments in which individuals let go of themselves and open up. At the same time, Protestant worship never intends to make captives or to seduce, but always offers the opportunity for critical distance. Mature Christians, who

---

13 Wilhelm Löhe, Agende für christliche Gemeinden des lutherischen Bekenntnisses, C. H. Becksche Buchhandlung, Nördlingen 1853, p. XIV.

accept their responsibility before God, celebrate the service here together – all of them as priestesses and priests. Reflection and contemplation are an essential part of Protestant spirituality.

13. The blessing

The service ends with a gesture for which the body and hands of the minister are only borrowed, for it is God who acts. Pastors promise the congregation something which they can in no way fulfil. They are a channel, a vessel, as they raise their hands and say, »The Lord bless you and keep you; the Lord make his face shine upon you and be gracious to you; the Lord lift up his countenance upon you and give you peace.« The gesture of blessing and the ancient Israelite benediction (Numbers 6:24–26) possibly demonstrate more clearly than anything else what grace is. We are not in a position to give ourselves security or to form our days. The benediction is the point at which we are most passive. We are observed, a strange face shines a light upon us, and in this light we are made real and transformed. We cannot ourselves produce vitality and healing, wholeness and peace; blessing is given to us by God.

It is not easy to receive blessing. It requires openness and the ability to let go. We do not ask about preconditions or how it works; we trust completely, letting ourselves fall into a promise. We enter into a life that is not justified by ourselves.

This takes place in stereotyped language, because the rigid formula goes beyond the understanding and belief of the subjects. It goes beyond thought. There is no more argument or controversy; blessing can only be received by undivided consent to God. We are integrated into God's affirmation of the world into which we will return as we pass through the door of the church.

14. The language of a church service

»The former descends, the latter ascends.« A special language expresses in the liturgy these contrary movements which are so decisive for Lutheran worship, this rhythmic pulse of receiving and responding, of hearing and speaking. One may call it a seeking language. It is entirely captivated by God's work and his word. It listens more than it speaks. It does not intend to convey information, but is speechless in the face of the unimaginable with which it is confronted in the presence of God. It wants to give testimony to that. What is spoken gives expression to a strong relationship that cannot be condensed into words and facts, but is a constantly fresh experience of the living God, a seeking and longing for him.

Nowadays, when Christians want to speak of God and their faith, they often find themselves in a strange dilemma: words quickly reach their limits just when they were beginning to mean something. They seem to be worn-out, even ideological. Just as the word »God« has been misused a thousand times over, so is it constantly misinterpreted and contaminated by self-interest. For me, this occurs more and more frequently: I have stepped up to the altar as minister, the open service book lies in front of me and the congregation at my back are waiting for my words, but suddenly I am no longer sure of my voice. I feel a prickling in the back of my neck, and I do not know whether I will be able to speak out loud. Instinctively,

I hesitate. What am I doing here? How should I pray distinctly, and what words should I use? »Let us …«, »Grant us, that …«, »Heavenly Father …«. Can I possibly go on using such rigid, hackneyed phraseology? Would it not be better to keep silent, to approach God wordlessly, indicating that words fail me and that I have no idea what I can say?

Many of the prayers I come across are full of well-worn metaphors, hollow semantic phrases, banal platitudes in churchy language. How often have prayers served as a cover-up! How much that was wrong has been justified in prayers! How often have believers made themselves comfortable in words that confirmed and reassured them and protected them from reality.

And there is another matter. The forest of language is becoming denser. In the thickets, modern-day examples of the human species sniff the air and automatically suspect that every new linguistic phenomenon conceals a trap; in this sceptical atmosphere, forms of religious language are in a difficult position. For at the present time, a certain understanding of verbal utterances is almost omnipresent. The philosopher of science Bruno Latour once called it »double-click communication«.[14] What does that mean? A word is in a sense the access code to a fact. Here is the word »table«, double-click: aha, it means a real table. Here comes the word »universe«, double-click: we look up to the sky. Aha, we are referring to an immeasurable space, far-reaching and unexplored. Now we find the word »God«, double-click: nothing. »There is no God that

---

14 Bruno Latour, Jubilieren, Über religiöse Rede, Suhrkamp Verlag, Berlin 2011, p. 34 ff.

›there is‹,« wrote Dietrich Bonhoeffer. So what kind of word is that? What is it good for, if it does not refer to a determinable fact of reality?

This peculiar gap left by the word »God« is quickly filled up by many Christians, because they feel that they would be driven into a corner, were they to bid farewell to this all-pervading »double-click« communication. Strange new linguistic coinages then come into being. The word »God«, double-click: »certain brain waves« or »a cipher for entirety of the world«. Indeed, many experienced church people stumble into this trap: the word »God«, double-click: »Aha, beneficial to mental health« or »precondition for happiness« or, especially popular: »God«, double-click: »guarantor of social values«.

But in more enlightened moments the believer hesitates. The word »God« comes up … and nothing is to be seen. Nothing is there which might be said to be authoritative. The word »God« actually undermines the widespread, apparently scientific double-click type of speaking. There is nothing to which the word refers, but at the same time there is not »nothing«, but rather something much larger than language and all the reality it depicts. Something which I have to enter as I speak, searching, using imagery, tentatively – and every time I find an expression, it tells me straightaway that it still does not say anything. Words of faith do not express »something«, in the sense of a factual description, but they are out looking, they are on the move. They are being tugged along, for the believing soul has fallen into a current which bears it in the direction of God.

Here we have a case of speaker's block, and that is in my opinion a godsend! It takes us back to the origins, where we had not formed a system of sentences and definitions. We must search for the words that fail us – and in that way our words gain poetry and spirituality.

Today's Christianity is in danger of presenting itself as one world view in the concert of competing ideological systems. Unfortunately, Christianity today largely gives the impression of being a plausible interpretation of the world, referring to the real facts, now clearly and reliably ordered in a Christian sense. It is as though one were able to speak of matters of faith just as one talks about economic or political developments or social justice. But that is incorrect and misleading: religious language does not explain, it seeks. Religious language widens the horizon, and does not make definitions. It is essentially poetic, not conceptual or even scientific. The church cannot speak like a political party or a particular interest group. The church's message, if one really wants to know, is not »something« to be found in the words, but the very nature of the words itself, their movement.

The language of the church service is ancient. In some of the formulations it can be traced back to the first utterances of the Christian faith, for example the Kyrie or the Creed. Yet at the same time, it is completely up to date and new. Here and now, the experience of God is realised in faith. Here and now, our words show that God is alive. Therefore, it does not help if we simply preserve and continue what has always been done and said in worship. Church services, their rites and their language, find their truth in the present time and in those places where we celebrate them. We also have to adopt and adapt traditions for ourselves today. We must rediscover what used to be, which will otherwise lose its meaning. It is always important to put traditions to the proof and see whether they meet the questions of the modern era. Church services tend to lead into a confined space, in which the insiders are only concerned with themselves and shut out the outside world.

But the opposite perspective is also correct. Every creative innovation in a worship service has to compare with the power of what has been handed down to us. New ideas and alterations need to be justified with respect to what has grown over the centuries.

In its various aspects, a church service resembles a river flowing towards the God who is coming. It consists of sources and waterfalls. The banks are solid and permanent, with their coves and rapids – rituals and biblical texts which have proved their worth over the centuries. In the course of time the river has meandered and made sudden breakthroughs to new forms. But it is the river in its entirety, with its origins and its constant movement, which forms the reality of worship. Old and new elements are inseparable. The forms which are preserved in the service books and the variations and new developments are complementary to each other.

15. Music in worship

The church service is rich in linguistic and sensual experience. It is not just the words – colours and vestments, the church interior and liturgical objects all play a specific role in the worship celebration. The sunlight coming through the windows, the smells in the church, the books and pictures, even the shadows, the woodworms and the carefully concealed clutter contribute to the event.

Protestant worship is particularly influenced by the music. The prayers are repeatedly expressed in chants and hymns, and the melody and harmony give space to emotions. In parts, this leads to the recollection of familiar tradition, while at other times new and surprising sounds may be heard. The organ and other instruments create resonances which open up alternative paths to internalisation and contemplation.

Music and church worship are closely connected. With their powerful and inexplicable effect, both of them make contact with spiritual areas of which humans are only partially aware or conscious. They touch places that language can hardly reach, and they delve into past impressions and memories. What cannot be expressed in words can become reality in music as rhythm and sound. Music is thus more than a mere enhancement of the power of words, and more than an intensified preaching. Like silence, it can become a particular way to encounter God.

16. »A moment now here and then gone«

Lutheran worship has always lived in the tension between creative innovation and attachment to tradition. This contrast has always been productive. Even the beginnings five hundred years ago had this twofold nature: cautious new approaches, but also the rediscovery and strengthening of continuity with the origins of Christian worship.

Today, in the ever-changing forms of recollection and memories, this tension has become acute. The past is seldom recalled in human memory, but rather stored by technical methods. Terms such as tradition and identity are becoming fragile. All kinds of events, down to family outings, are captured on photos, videos, sound recordings or in scanned documents.

These supposedly objective memories are permanently available and overpower those who would like to relive the feelings in their memory, to recall the emotional experience. Since identity is essentially dependent upon the arrangement and selection of recollections that pass before my inner eye and form my personality, it is now difficult to recognise what is »identifiable«. Tradition has become a permanent topic when it comes to Protestant discussions about worship.

Memory has a dynamic that undermines predictability. It happens suddenly; from one moment to the next, everything appears in a new light. Friedrich Nietzsche formulated this precisely: »And it is a matter for wonder: a moment now here and then gone, nothing before it came, again nothing after it is gone, nonetheless returns as a ghost and disturbs the peace of a later moment. A leaf flutters from the scroll of time, floats away – and suddenly floats back again and falls into the man's lap. Then the man says, ›I remember‹ …«[15] When seen in this way, memory is one of the essential sources of every innovation, and there is a danger of stagnation wherever the »wonder« of the return of the past is prevented.

In the interests of innovation and modern-day relevance, it is necessary to insist more strongly than ever before on the maintenance of tradition. We must hold on to an awareness of the fact that past and future development is part of the human condition, even if this seems to be threatened at present. Thus, it is one of our most important tasks to ensure that the »ordinary services«, the normal weekly Sunday services in the

---

15 Friedrich Nietzsche, On the uses and disadvantages of history for life, in: Untimely Meditations, Cambridge University Press, New York 1997, p. 61.

church year as shaped by the traditions of the Lutheran churches and the local congregations, should be upheld and continuously evolved. They should regain the right balance over against the manifold special forms of worship that determine our ecclesial life today.

17. In conclusion: Luther's ribald language

What is the worship service? Above all, it represents a transformation which is not to be expressed in words. Whether miserable or magnificent, quiet or festive, boring or gripping – in every case something happens which we can only feel and understand to a limited extent.

Martin Luther, who gave absolute priority to sermon and sacraments, was able to describe the all-too-human side of the church service in a kind of caricature. He knows very well that the miracle of the divine presence can take place in the most insignificant, modest or unsuccessful places. In his Table Talk we find a short conversation after a Sunday service: »Cum uxor sua diceret [When his wife said]: ›Indeed, sir, the church was so full that it stank‹, respondit Lutherus [Luther answered]: ›There was many a heap of filth inside, even if well concealed, and it is all for the best that they have been carried outside again, etc.‹«[16]

---

[16] »Cum uxor sua diceret [Als seine Frau sagte]: Ey, herr, es war so vol in der kirchen, das es stanck, respondit Lutherus [antwortete Luther]: Es ist auch mancher guther hauffen dreck drinnen gewesen, wie wol verborgen, und ist das beste daran, das sie ihn wider außgetragen haben etc.« WA TR 2,2563b. Translation: Williamson.

Martin Kumlehn

Church for the People

Guidelines for Protestant Parish Work

1. Welcome!

It is a bright sunny day in the late summer in a North American university town. I decide to go to the conference venue on foot, passing hotels, banks and restaurants. A spacious park lies next to a residential and commercial building, and there is a constant stream of traffic on the road next to me. I walk from block to block, going past schools and museums. Suddenly I can see a large banner in front of me, hanging over the sidewalk from a church doorway: »Welcome,« it says, »... wherever you are on your spiritual journey.«

Ever since then, this momentary impression has summed up for me my dream and ideal of a church

- which is open, yet remains true to itself and its own purpose,
- which has a specific place, a building, a character,
- whose doors are unlocked, both literally and in the figurative sense,
- which offers people a community where they can find a religious interpretation of life in narrative and ritual practice, but without any compulsion.

Such a church is realistic enough to assume that it is not only within its walls that people seek answers to the whys and wherefores of their lives and try to get in touch with the sources of their existence. This church knows that many people are already concerned with the spiritual and religious dimension of their lives in their social contexts, both public and private, and especially in the context of very challenging experiences and biographical turning points. The Protestant church cultivates the communicative and ritual ways of expressing this dimension of meaning in life and warmly welcomes all those who are looking for orientation and assurance on their spiritual journey through life and continually want to find a new foundation in faith.

2. How it all began – on the road with Jesus

Even before the first Christian communities came into being, people who were in contact with Jesus of Nazareth had exactly this experience: his words and actions made them aware of their closeness to God on their spiritual journey through life. They heard and felt God's unconditional concern and care (Mt 6:25 ff.), regardless of whether they or their fellow humans felt that they deserved it. This was the gospel proclaimed by Jesus (see Mark 1:14 f.), the good news (Greek: *euangelion*) of God's steadfast promise to accompany every person on the path through life, to care for their souls and to open up the kingdom of heaven to them. Jesus was able to illustrate this in the form of stories and parables (see Lk 15:11 ff. and Mt 13:44 f.). His message fell on fertile ground.

The wonderfully liberating power of this message was manifested in a series of confessions, conversions and healings of the body and soul (Lk 19:1 ff.; Mt 15:21 ff.). It became entrenched in the heart of Jesus' listeners, forming them into a community of women and men who spread the gospel, the good news of the »infinite worth of every single human soul« (Adolf von Harnack) and tried to live their lives accordingly. Even this first small band of followers, people with very different social and religious biographies, experienced a degree of recognition and esteem, loyalty and fellowship, such as they had never known hitherto.

After the brutal death of Jesus, the founder and midpoint of their community, the disciples stayed together. In spite of the great disappointment and deep despondency which had seized them, they soon realised that everything they had experienced with Jesus and all that they had learned from him about himself and about God was by no means dependent on the physical presence of the Nazarene. On the contrary, the newly gained perspectives of hope continued to work in and among them. They felt that in particular whenever they reminded themselves of his words and deeds and celebrated the Lord's Supper together in remembrance of him.

This is the subject of the Easter legends, of which the story of the two disciples on the road to Emmaus is perhaps the most impressive. The risen Lord joined them on their journey, although they did not at first recognise him (see Luke 24:13 ff.). The two travellers talk to their companion about the great expectations they had set in Jesus and they speak openly of their profound disappointment at his death. In their confusion and dismay they tell him about the empty grave the women had found when they went to anoint the body of the crucified one. Angels had appeared to them, saying that he was alive. But no-one had seen him … After this, their new companion enters the conversation and tries to demonstrate to them by interpretation of the scriptures that Jesus had to suffer all this and rise from the dead. But it is in vain: they do not recognise him. When they arrive in Emmaus, it is already early evening, and the two invite the unknown traveller to stay with them. They sit down at the table to share an evening meal. And suddenly, as he takes the bread, blesses and breaks it, their eyes are opened and they recognise him – and he immediately vanishes. And then they remember how they had been moved on their journey, as the risen Jesus had tried to comfort them with the help of words from the Bible: »Were not our hearts burning within us while he was talking to us on the road, while he was opening the scriptures to us?«

The legend of the Emmaus disciples is a key narrative for the understanding of church and local congregation. Because it illustrates the essential motives and factors leading to their foundation:

1) The story is about a meeting on the road leading to an invitation: »Stay with us!« – The Christian community develops between companions who have been abandoned. On their common path through life, they believe and feel that the risen Jesus is alongside them – an experience that calls for a pause and some shelter in company, that is to say, for a place to stay in the daily life of the world.
2) The Emmaus disciples cannot keep their own experience and their friends' reports to themselves. They are compelled to tell the stranger about it, discuss it with him, and ask what it all means for them and the hopes they had had. – The Christian community proves to be a community that tells its stories. The stories and legends recorded in the Gospels tell of the spiritual experiences that people have made in their en-

counter with Jesus of Nazareth. Even later, people always talk of such experiences when they come into contact with the gospel through the church's preaching. Those who hear and believe in the good news are able to speak about their trust and their doubts, about liberation and fear – and similar accounts are already to be found in biblical stories and legends. Spiritual experiences that shape the history of one's life can be clarified and interpreted when they are projected into the stories that are already told in the Bible. In this way, everyone's own life story echoes biblical narratives, whilst the ancient tales are revived by the parallels to present-day biographical experiences.

3) This echo created by narratives helps to recall what always worked in the past, in new and different ways: to remind oneself of God, the basis and origin of trust. This is the elementary religious act of the Christian faith. »Religion« (Latin: *religio*) literally means »reconnection«. It takes place when those associated with one another in the narrative community of Christians remind each other when, where and how they became aware that they were wonderfully accompanied, cared for, safeguarded. – The Christian church is a community of memories.
4) Alongside the narration, there are rites which offer assurance of meaning: the rituals of baptism, benediction and the Lord's Supper re-enact the experience of recognition and esteem, of belonging and fellowship, that was once shared with Jesus and has meanwhile been brought back to life again and again, and continues to do so: »Do this in remembrance of me.« (1 Cor 11:24) – The Christian church is a community of rites.

These four characteristics distinguish the church and the local congregation to this day and make them recognisable as a Christian community. The ritual of baptism is the basis of church membership. The practice of Christian life is based on the biblical narratives, which are remembered as explanations and interpretations of living faith and are celebrated in worship. The church sees itself as companionship on the road, constantly moving on, on the rise, already nourished in this world by the strength of the world to come (see Heb 13:14).

3. Community of the baptised

The real founding legend of the church can be found in Acts, more precisely in Luke's Pentecost story. It tells how Jesus' promise to his disciples was fulfilled: »You will receive power when the Holy Spirit has come upon you; and you will be my witnesses in Jerusalem, in all Judea and Samaria, and to the ends of the earth.« (Acts 1:8) Luke describes the sending of the Spirit as a dramatic event, accompanied by »a sound like the rush of a violent wind«. Tongues of fire rested on the heads of the apostles when, filled with the Holy Spirit, they begin to preach in all sorts of languages – »as the Spirit gave them ability,« Luke notes explicitly (Acts 2:4).

The scene described reminds one of the mythological story of the Tower of Babel (Gen 11). There it says at the beginning: »Now the whole earth had one language and the same words.« Then people decided to build a tower »with its top in the heavens, and let us make a name for ourselves«. But God prevented the storming of heaven by confusing the language of the tower builders, so that people were no longer able to understand one another and the great community project could not be carried out. This story forms the narrative background for the Pentecost miracle depicted by Luke: the people »from every nation under heaven« who had come to Jerusalem for the feast heard the apostles »speaking in the native language of each … about God's deeds of power«. (Acts 2:8ff.) The whole world hears and understands the message. For it is directed to all people and all nations. The Pentecost legend emphasises the global significance of Jesus' preaching about God's closeness, as well as the universal implications of his death and resurrection.

As Peter goes on to preach a sermon, he interprets these events as the fulfilment of ancient prophetic promises. It ends in the confession »that God has made him both Lord and Messiah, this Jesus whom you crucified« (Acts 2:36). Through baptism in the name of Jesus Christ for the forgiveness of sins, one may receive the gift of the Holy Spirit, share in the Christ event and be received into the Christian community, the realm of Christ (see Acts 2:38). Thus, another ritual emerges alongside the shared meal – baptism as a ritual of transition and initiation. Whoever is baptised belongs to Christ, who has brought salvation – the forgiveness of sins – through his death on the cross (see Rom 6:3ff.). Whoever is baptised belongs to the Christian community. As a result, baptism becomes a distinguishing feature, first of all within the Jewish community in the Temple or the synagogues, but later on in opposition to it. Step by step, the Christian community gradually evolves from an inner-Jewish group to an independent religious community. This is a complicated and sometimes quite painful process. For a long time, the newly emerged religious community wrestled with the position of traditional Jewish rituals (for example circumcision and fasting) within it. From the very beginning, and ultimately down to the present day, there has been theological controversy regarding the relationship of Christianity to God's promises and commandments recorded in the five books of Moses (Torah) and the other scriptures of the Hebrew Bible (see Romans 9–11).

The Christian church – each one in its own place – is the fellowship of those baptised in the name of Jesus Christ. This fellowship, then as now, seeks to model its faith and life on the teachings and life of Jesus, to live together with mutual concern for the needs of body and soul, to celebrate worship services together, and to join in taking care of the spiritual dimension of human existence in the practice of meditation and prayer (see Acts 2:42).

From the outset, the local fellowships have been places where life was interpreted religiously in the light of the gospel. Here people experience release from sin and bondage; here every person's unique significance is respected; here forms of activity are developed to increase solidarity. For the good news helps to find a meaning of life which provides liberation from anxiety, selfishness and unkindness. The local church as a group of travelling companions issues an invitation to share life together for a certain time. It is a community of story-telling and rites, offering places, times, rituals, liturgies, narratives and symbols that are used and shared, narrated and debated in common. It promotes the exchange of experiences and encourages people to talk about their own life stories. The task and the specific message of the church also consists in bringing people to find confidence in the meaning of life, enabling them as followers of Jesus to give shape to their freedom in a way that suits them. Under certain circumstances, however, this can also mean that an individual Christian practises this freedom without maintaining constant contact with the local congregation. This may seem problematic in the eyes of those who feel particularly attached to church life and are actively involved in parish work, but it is fully in accordance with the institutional, functional nature of the church. For the church is not an end in itself, but merely the intermediary of the good news. In other words, church and congregation do not exist for their own sake, but for the sake of their message, which is to be passed on to people. This basic insight, which is firmly anchored in the confessions of the Protestant churches, helps to ensure that local parishes do not look disparagingly or even discriminatorily at Christians who believe and act outside the official church. A look at the origins of the Christian church reveals that the relationship between individual faith and organised Christianity has always been controversial.

4. Plurality of local church forms

The first Christians came together as a kind of association, a group of religiously like-minded people who met up in private homes to celebrate the Lord's Supper. The »home« as the site of liturgical life came to replace the former locations for worship – Temple and synagogue. As a result, it is the house church which is dominant in the New Testament depictions of the earliest Christian congregations, even when using the word »church« (Greek: *ekklesia*).

It is always the congregation of one town that gathers in the house of one or other of its members (see Romans 16:5; 1 Cor 16:19; Col 4:15). To be sure, more and more other forms of religious communion emerged as well. In the course of Christianity's missionary outreach, forms of community developed which had a sectarian nature, particularly in the cities, and were characterised by a high degree of commitment in doctrine and life. Apart from the organisational form of the house church, there were other types of social structure which were either more strongly oriented towards the Jewish synagogues or modelled on schools of philosophy or mystery cults. As a result, in the first three centuries of the Christian era there was no uniform social form of church, but different types of community existed parallel to one another. The Christian religion was at that time neither systematically organised nor territorially structured and was not yet in a position to establish a social form that was binding on all Christians.

This changed in the course of the so-called Constantinian shift in the fourth century, when the hitherto persecuted Christian religion became the Roman state religion. Now organisational issues were of paramount importance for church leadership, and a new type of local church community began to emerge: the parish (from the Greek *ta paroika*, meaning »neighbouring«). In the strictly hierarchically structured organisation of the Roman Catholic Church, the parish denotes the territorial jurisdiction of a priest. The German word »Pfarrer« is derived from that. However, according to Roman Catholic canon law, the local church is by no means identical with the district of a priest. Rather, the diocese is the authoritative church organisation, which is now divided into parishes by the ruling bishop in order to guarantee the regular execution of church activities. Thus, the Catholic »parish« does not originally represent a »congregation« in the sense of an independent ecclesiastical social form, but rather an administrative district of the diocese.

Nonetheless, the parish or local church proved to be the form of church organisation that has lasted down to the present day. It is the assembly of Christians who live more or less by chance in a certain place or district in analogy to the secular state structures. As a rule, this assignment to one's home town or village is easy to understand and poses no problem to most people. This is especially true, given that everyone is naturally free to attend events in a different parish, for example the neighbouring one. It is always possible, after all, to apply for membership of a different parish, if desired. In addition, in Germany church communities which go beyond the traditional parish boundaries have already existed for a long time. During the period of Pietism in the eighteenth century and the revivalist movements in the nineteenth century, home prayer circles and special interest groups enjoyed a renaissance. Examples for this are the house groups or the regional independent evangelical associations (»Landeskirchliche Gemeinschaften«). Particularly in large conurbations, the open churches and city churches now play an important role. There are churches specialising in art and culture as well as long-term social and charitable projects that have a parochial character.

5. Institution of freedom – turning points of the Reformation

»The church is the church only when it exists for others.« (Dietrich Bonhoeffer) This principle makes it impossible for churches to remain introspective. The church is not there for its own sake, but for the sake of the people. With this insight – together with its practical consequences – the church realises the concept of the doctrine of justification for itself. For a church that does not exist for itself, but only for others, has to take account of the fact that the Christian faith means liberation from worry about oneself. This has to be reflected in its self-understanding and its organisational forms, so that it is capable of leading an active life of trust and of communicating this trust to others.

As the church is in this sense freed from itself, it is free for others and leaves others free to live their faith in direct relationship with God. The church has therefore been rightly called the »institution of freedom« (Trutz Rendtorff).

The idea of an institution can already be found in the context of the Augsburg Confession of 1530, which is still authoritative for the Protestant church today. Its author Melanchthon deliberately chose a concept of the church that was not based on substance, but on function. Church is not defined by a specific form, but by a specific task. In order to be »freely justified for Christ's sake through faith,« (Article 4 of the Augsburg Confession), »the Ministry of Teaching the Gospel and administering the Sacraments was instituted (Latin: *institutum est*). For through the Word and Sacraments, as through instruments (Latin: *instrumenta*), the Holy Ghost is given, who works faith where and when it pleases God in them that hear the Gospel« (Article 5). In thus addressing the Protestants, Melanchthon emphasised most firmly that the office of preaching and the church itself have a functional, instrumental character. Their value and significance lies in the fact that they are means and tools, tools for propagating the Christian religion, the gospel – which works faith where and when God pleases. While the Christian message is offered as a proposal in worship services, religious instruction and counselling, it is not possible to determine how it will be accepted by the church or by individuals. If a person discovers something in this message which affects his or her own life, this is experienced as a gift of God through the Holy Spirit.

In its own understanding, the Protestant church applies the Reformation insight of the doctrine of justification in a certain sense to its own self. Just as individual people cannot of their own will come to trust in the positive sense of their existence and of the world they live in, so is the church unable to provide evidence of faith. Whatever it does, whatever images and symbols it employs in order to present people with the gospel in the cause of self-analysis, it always remains dependent on the divine self-manifestation or, to put it in other words, on the individual's adaptation of traditional forms of meaning. In this way, as it attempts to explain religion, the church expresses the fact that meaning is not at our disposal. Even beyond that: by indicating that identity and existential security are not at our disposal, that is to say, by articulating the transcendental relationships of life, the church conveys to society a critical principle which prevents it from considering the cultural and creative possibilities of this world as absolute. Religion and the church keep this memory alive: that the way of life of an individual or of society as a whole can only be freely developed if it is anchored in the consciousness of a transcendent origin and basis for identity and the world.

The understanding of the church as institutional and functional was accompanied in Protestant Christianity from the beginning by high regard for the local church. In Protestantism, religious life is on principle not organised »top down«, but »bottom-up«, not by the entire church or a regional district, but by the one congregation. At a comparatively early stage, Martin Luther was convinced »that a Christian assembly or congregation has the right and power to judge all teaching and to call, appoint, and dismiss teachers. Established and proven by Scripture,« as he entitled a treatise in 1523 in which he was principally interested in strengthening the rights of the local congregation over against the bishop and ultimately against Rome. In his argumentation, however, Luther concentrated on the main priority of preaching the word. According to Luther, the autonomy of the congregation consisted primarily in the appointment of pastors and the order of worship, while, for example, the ordination of the pastors and the visitation of the individual local churches should continue to fall within the remit of a higher level in the church system. It is by no means necessary to draw the conclusion that even in the Reformation the larger organisation of the church took hierarchical precedence over the single parish. Quite the opposite is true: the Christian church, which is confessed in the Creed, is for Luther the »communion of saints« and thus primarily represented by individuals united in worship and in daily life. Individual Christians join together in hearing the Word of God and breaking bread, and in this gathering they form the church. Incidentally, this fully corresponds to the understanding of the church in the Augsburg Confession, the central document of the Protestant churches, in which Melanchthon develops the true nature of the church from its commitment to the teaching of the gospel (see Articles 4, 5 and 7). The Reformation abolishes the medieval hierarchy. The local church is no longer the lowest element in the hierarchy of ecclesiastical authorities, but in principle the only one. The congregation is, so to speak, the original and basic form of church. It consciously and explicitly orientates itself to those communicative conditions which ensure that individuals find meaning in their lives – and it therefore continues to be of inestimable value for the communication of the Christian faith today.

7. Religion in practice

The widespread need to see one's own life from a religious perspective, that is to say, to find symbols, interpretations and rituals for relevant questions of life which are able to articulate all that is fundamental and absolute, depends to a great extent on experiences of local religious practice. For these challenge one to cast a religious light on one's own life, even if the symbolism, explanations and forms of worship specifically offered seem to be out of place or do not (any longer) find our acceptance.

They do, in fact, awaken the longing for a religious interpretation of life's meaning. To be sure, that is also the case for other cultural media, such as the cinema, literature, fine arts, print media, television, internet, and especially radio and streaming services. In many different ways these media communicate the fact that life does not just happen, but that one is always seeking for an interpretation of events. But there is one significant difference between the interpretations of life and meaning offered by the media and the communication organised by the church: the Evangelical Church in Germany (EKD) has a specific public presence of exactly 14,055 congregations organised in twenty regional churches totalling 21,922,000 members (official statistic of the EKD as of 31 December 2016). At times when the public sphere exists almost exclusively in the media, and is thus mostly experienced in a virtual form, the social space of a church congregation gains a unique significance, because it enables physical communication and personal interaction, something which is becoming increasingly rare. However, both are essential for the religious interpretation of meaning, which for more and more individuals is developing into an inner process; orientation on the meaning of life is no longer available externally with the aid of traditionally unquestioned certainties. In the course of this internalisation of the grounds for certainty, people become increasingly aware that confidence in meaning and its credibility are never completely covered by the words, symbols, rituals and gestures with which they are expressed. In order to make such individual assurances religiously valid, the church and the congregation do well to provoke and promote them by presenting concrete forms and positions of traditional Christian exposition and to support them with stable, institutionalised offers of religious communication and interpretation.

8. Lively diversity – diverse participation

In the last few decades, parish life has gained considerably in profile and plurality, which can only be welcomed from a Protestant point of view. People can take part in many ways in the church's activities for the interpretation of life. Some are intensively involved in »their« parish, identifying themselves strongly with what the local church offers; others only take advantage of them from time to time. For many people, church membership does not have very much practical significance, while others understand and experience church activities as an important element in their way of life. That is why there are now various ways of participating in church life. One can pursue the Christian interpretation of life in the church together with others in regular groups and circles or just in special situations, such as transition periods or moments of crisis. For some church members, this is the type of participation which corresponds to their religious needs; this explains why they are apparently hesitant, watching from the sidelines, in spite of the diversity of activities offered by the church, but that often does not really say a great deal about their relationship to church and congregation. Even if active participation in local church life is not an option for them, they often appreciate the fact that such opportunities for participation exist. This is confirmed by the empirical membership surveys conducted by the Evangelical Church in Germany (EKD), which have been repeated every few years in the last half-century. This is why there is much to suggest that those who participate in the church are not in competition with members of the local parish, but are rather complementary to them.

Nationwide surveys of church members also show that there are now active forms of church life that are not determined by the local congregation, but rather organised in a flexible kind of fellowship. Nowadays there are many different ways of practising one's faith in a temporary community. And the Evangelical Church in Germany (EKD) rightly responds to this with the programmatic demand that the Church should present itself today as a matter of principle as »open and welcoming, bearing responsibility for the world and culture-oriented« (»Kirche der Freiheit«, 44) in order to meet such expectations and needs. Above all, it must finally abandon the apparently ineradicable but erroneous notion held both by committed and by sceptical people, that regular attendance at certain church activities is indispensable for genuine Christianity. It is also time to extend the call for »lively church life« in the direction of »church with others«. In that case, merely occasional participation in church-related events would no longer be regarded as inadequate, and church members acting in this way would no longer have a guilty conscience. If those working for the church were to focus more on the needs of the »occasional Christians« as well as of the so-called »non-denominationals«, then they would not see much of a problem in the fact that many people only come into contact with the church for the service on Christmas Eve or at the funeral of a neighbour. Incidentally, it is also possible to observe very different levels of attachment to the church among those members who are more committed. This is reflected not least in the diversity of church-related activities in various groups and circles. Here it is possible to distinguish at least three forms of participation: active commitment measured by regular visits to Sunday morning service, attendance at a weekly discussion group and/or Bible study meeting, and membership of the parish council. Occasional visits to the Senior Citizens' afternoon, involvement in the »One World Group«, confirmation classes, visiting a discussion evening on embryo research, the youth camp and the annual church fête are examples for »temporary community«, while participation at a funeral or a church wedding, visiting the nativity play on Christmas Eve, using the services of the diaconal nurse or the parish social service centre may all be reckoned as sporadic participation in local church life, in each case motivated by a particular situation in a personal biography or the time of year. As already mentioned, it can also be observed in the recent past that alternative forms of »temporary community« alongside the local parishes have come into being, especially in the larger cities –

for example Art Churches or City Churches, Rooms of Silence or Kirchentage (Christian rallies). This shows more and more that »lively church« and »church for others« are no longer alternatives. On the contrary, precisely because people of different origins, interests and biographies come together for a certain time in the church to work on specific projects and topics, they bring both of these motives together.

9. Occasional church

There is much to be said in favour of regarding the church as an institution – comparable to a family, to the legal system or sport. Incidentally, this could help the church to exist in the best Protestant sense, without looking anxiously at the statistics on visitors or members all the time. The family remains an institution, even though fewer and fewer people are living in families. In a similar way, one does not constantly call on the legal system with its courts, lawyers and prosecutors, but it is there – »Thank God« – when needed.

The church must not be seen as a special place to go to in order to practise a more or less ecclesiastical life, but as an institution, a place to be visited on occasion – that is to say, when one is in need of it. A church that is sensitive to the expectations of its members – as well as to those outside its walls – and consistently reacts to their needs is cast in the mould of an »occasional church« (Michael Nüchtern). This means that church services for special occasions, for example at the beginning of life (baptism), in the transition to adulthood (confirmation), when tying the knot (marriage ceremony) and passing away (funeral service), appear to be the hidden paradigm of church life. For they offer an opportunity to interpret and experience present, past and future life. This space, with its respective rituals as the case arises, is opened up by the institution church, creating social commitment and opportunities for interpretation which help those concerned, together with their relations and friends, to face death, to enter into a lasting partnership, to welcome new life or to accept responsibility and blessing for adult life. Other than at these transitional stages of life, there are naturally further possibilities to come into contact with the church. Such »docking stations« might be the first day at school or a stay in hospital, the celebration of the 50th anniversary of confirmation, marking the start of retirement, the inauguration of a new sports centre or an adult education function offered by the church. The spectrum of »opportunities« could easily be extended; there is a certain understanding of religion and church which considers every kind of religious communication to be basically based on an occasion, since it is always embedded in a specific context, a situation experienced by an individual. If that were not the case, it would be simply futile.

If one accepts that religion is linked to a particular context, then it is possible to take a broader view of »congregation«, extending it to church events characterised by a more »restricted, project-oriented and situational involvement«.[17] At the same time, this could help the parish to counteract its social structure, which is often organised on the lines of a club and tends to be restricted to people from a certain background.

---

17 https://www.kirche-im-aufbruch.ekd.de/downloads/kirche-der-freiheit.pdf, p. 54.

This is more necessary than ever, since it has become quite clear for some time that the individualisation of neighbourhoods and lifestyles in modern-day society has led to an increased interest in a lasting, stable experience of community. However, opportunities for an open parish life allowing the individual to experience sustainable community in an atmosphere of mutual trust also contain certain risks. If the parish has an idealised image of itself as a place where community succeeds and perfect harmony prevails, then it may well happen that the real-life ambiguity and dichotomy of modern religious thought, and in particular the tangible conflicts between differing religious positions and individual lifestyles, are taken to be unjustified *a priori*. Controversies are then ruled out, and religious ideals such as charity and brotherhood mutate unexpectedly to instruments of domination employed to cover up conflicts of interests which really exist: differences are glossed over, people of dissenting views are muzzled, and whatever is unfamiliar or strange is ignored. Implying that the church is a conflict-free zone in the midst of a society marked by conflict and competition means that the compulsion to join the community and the pressure on individuals to conform is intensified.

The multifarious local church has a broad palette of offers and many options for participation, whilst above all recognizing that people may basically keep their distance; this is the social form of church that is appropriate for modern, differentiated Protestantism. It gives people space to appropriate Christianity individually and organically combines individual forms of piety with commonly maintained religious lifestyles into group cultures within the congregation. For this reason it is right to be critical of church growth strategies which are based on the assumption that the liberal church mentality of an »occasional church« is an inadequate form of Christianity or even a directly unchristian attitude. Under this false assumption, the church as an institution is often itself the object of missionary church growth. One should counter this criticism of the church with the truly Protestant assertion that an open church is not dependent on the participation of all its members in church life but rather – vice versa – that the parish itself should adjust to all those who belong to the church.

In addition, there should be serious consideration in future about how the institution church can succeed in not being perceived by the general public merely as an interest group for its members, but as an organisation that is basically responsible for religion. In this context, other forms of church affiliation must also be discussed. So far, church membership has been acquired through baptism. Will there be some kind of »tiered membership« in the future, for instance for those belonging to the local church support group or participating in church-based refugee work? Baptism is in most cases understood and practised as a family tradition. It therefore makes sense to pave the way for alternative possibilities of affiliation or membership in the church – especially given that tradition is breaking down generally.

The concept of a church based on multi-facetted local congregations will remain the primary option of Protestant Christianity for the foreseeable future. The gospel is for all people, all classes and lifestyles. Certainly there are lifestyles that are more in tune with church religion and others that are more remote. However, for the sake of the universality of its message the church must be keenly interested in appealing to all social milieus and lifestyles. Its future viability depends essentially on a success in continuing to function as a public social institution that takes responsibility for religion. The basic threefold practice of Protestant religiosity – hearing, interpretation and belief – is certainly not bound to a particular social form, but the notion of being an institution guarantees for generations to come the survival potential of the church that proclaims the gospel.

10. Church as a resource for the religious interpretation of life

It is typical for people living in modern society that they are not constantly accompanied by religious experiences and interpretations. Nowadays the practice of Christian faith has rather been shifted to unusual situations and experiences outside the daily, run of the mill routine. It is on the one hand the moments of joy and happiness, and on the other hand transition periods, disruptions and catastrophes which call for religious expression and religious interpretation. This applies not only to the experiences and destiny of individuals, but also to collective life experience. Events such as the tsunami on Boxing Day 2004 or the terrorist attack on a Christmas market in Berlin in 2016 make this clear.

Religion is the attempt to cope with the contingency, the apparent randomness of our existence and that of the world in which we live, in an interpretative and ritual way. Its cultural function consists in interpreting life to reveal its meaning: »Where do I come from? Where am I going to? What is the meaning of my existence?« And above all, »What can you do when there is nothing you can do?«

This is where religion comes in. It opens up a perspective on life that does not prove itself in what is visible or possible; instead it reckons with what is not to be expected or constructed, and thus helps one to lead one's own life against the background of the God-concept, trusting that everything has a meaning, precisely when there is nothing more that can be done. However, such trust is always endangered and by no means self-evident. It is and remains fundamentally not at our disposal: the question of meaning is particularly acute when something terrible, unexpected, or brutal happens, but also when reconstructing one's own life story in search of coherence and meaning. At this point, people are still searching today – particularly intensively nowadays, I believe – for the spiritual sources of their existence, asking about the meaning of their lives. And it is not unusual for them to find it. Here is an example:

Eugen Ruge's novel »In Times of Fading Light« is the story of a family shaped by the ideals of communism and its attempts to deal with the fall of the GDR for their personal lives. One of the main characters of the novel, Alexander, remembers his religious conversion experience, »his own difficult, crazy, violent confrontation with that very subject the winter before, the winter of the millennium year, when everything broke apart for him and the birds – literally – fell from heaven. He tries to remember it: the moment when it – and yes, *what* exactly? – touched him or turned to him or made itself known? He doesn't know now. The moment eludes memory, he recollects only time before and after it, he remembers how for days (days?) he lay on the floorboards of some derelict house, helplessly following the way the pain ate at him from inside; he remembers the darkness, his sore hip bones – and he remembers, after it, the sense of release, of insight, he remembers how one morning he came out into the backyard with the warm ash-can in his hand, how he stood there and looked up, and how he saw it: up there in the black branches of a backyard poplar. Body chemistry? Downright lunacy? Or a moment of enlightenment? For days after that, he had gone around the streets with a deranged smile, every rusty streetlamp had looked to him miraculous, the mere sight of the yellow trains rattling their way along the stretch of overhead track above Schönhäuser Allee set off feelings of happiness, and in the eyes of the children who surrounded him, the smiling man, looking into his face without inhibition, he had seen it more than once: something for which he, brought up an atheist, had no term available to him.« (Ruge, 171)

The church, as a narrative community, would be exactly called upon to help to put such experiences into words. For people who have experienced something like this are in need of words which help them to interpret and comprehend their experience as religious events, illuminated by images of God in biblical texts. However, this presupposes that »the spaces offered by the church are not perceived just as media of community building, but as resources for accompanying individuals through their life and revealing its meaning to them«, as the impulse paper of the Council of the EKD formulated some time ago.[18]

When putting existential experiences into words, the church can borrow cultural expressions which attempt to give assurance of meaning, as long as it handles them with care, sensibility and curiosity. These symbols of meaning can be

18 https://www.kirche-im-aufbruch.ekd.de/downloads/kirche-der-freiheit.pdf, p. 42.

found wherever people establish a relationship to their own lives. It is more important than ever to take note of such symbols, to adopt and interpret them, to set them – usually critically – in relationship to one's own interpretation according to biblical tradition and testimonies of faith, and to integrate them into the communicative process of the various fields of action in the church. It is not a question of trying to ingratiate oneself with people, but rather to make it clear that questions of meaning are always religious questions in the end, when they concern the human being existentially and absolutely. Popular music in particular finds words to describe existential basic experiences, hopes and longings, which is also true in the biblical context, for example in the psalms. Many pop songs are basically modern psalms, confessions, entreaties, prayers – that is to say, religion, even though there is often no explicit reference to God. They often distance themselves deliberately from traditional religion, its practices, narratives and concepts, yet they cannot refrain from using images from religious language: »Himmel auf« (Silbermond), »Einer dieser Steine« (Sido feat. Mark Forster), »Haus am See« (Peter Fox), »I still haven't found what I'm looking for« (U2), »Wolke 7« (Max Herre feat. Philipp Poisel), »Ist da Jemand« (Adel Tawil).

A church that registers such symbols for the meaning of life and understands them as expressions of self-reassurance in the service of life, seeks to come into dialogue with its contemporaries by means of preaching and pastoral care, public relations or funerals, church services for first-year pupils or columns in the newspaper. To be sure, the church is aware that these people have long been believers and doubters, and that they were always on a spiritual journey through life. Nevertheless, given the background of its own language and religious rituals, it ventures – for its own sake – to carry this belief and doubt over into an open space of interpretation in which the power of the Christian faith can take effect as trust in the transcendental meaning of life.

12. Church as a companion

For many people in Germany, church occupies this position – it is an important player within the social framework of interest groups, agencies for meaning, and welfare organisations. Together with the institution »school« for education and the institution »medicine« for health, the church counts as part of public welfare services. This means that the very nature and appearance of the church has been thoroughly misunderstood if it is regarded as a unique kind of social form, isolated from other spheres of life. It is necessary to look at the church from the point of view of those functional tasks for individuals or for society as a whole which it accepts and performs – or refuses.

The church is primarily required and expected to perform services of a charitable, advisory, supportive and pastoral nature, as well as – albeit to a lesser extent – those that relate to education and ethical values. On the other hand, those services which the local church often regards as being central to its activities are not the ones that mainly interest the general public. The (weekly) Sunday church service and the presentation of religious or theological questions only appear relevant in the context of specific life problems, especially when individuals are trying to make sense of personal biographical crises or turning points.

It is not difficult to recognize that nowadays the church is principally appreciated and called upon when it appears useful in practical life. From a sociological perspective, these useful services of the church can be described as a helpful accompaniment in crises and at critical stages of life. Such accompaniment in crisis situations is probably seen by most people today as the main task of the church. That may even seem plausible for the multitude of fellow citizens who go to church once a year on Christmas Eve, because it helps many a family to master the precarious challenge of staging the Christmas festivities as a »celebration of love«. On the other hand, in recent decades, there has been a sharp decline in the expectations of the public at large with regard to the church's contribution to the representation and communication of values, especially in matters relating to practical life and education. At the most, the opinion of theology and the church might be sought when it comes to certain difficult issues concerning society in general, for example ethical problems of war and peace, environmental destruction or euthanasia. By contrast, the church's models of life interpretation and orientation are held to be largely irrelevant for the specific explanation and guidance of life. Nevertheless, the longing for a religious interpretation and orientation of a person's life has grown noticeably in recent years – and that is precisely why it is necessary to ask why the churches are so seldom successful in satisfying these heightened demands for interpretations and practices which are both lucid and comprehensible.

13. Church and social media

In this context, social networks also play an important role as modern forms of communitisation, whose characteristic features are individual choice, overcoming distance through technology and mostly short-time contacts. Similarly to other institutions, such as politics, law, the state, friendship and family, churches and local congregations are currently in a process of considerable transformation, not least because of the emergence of the new media. However, whether or not this heralds the end of the church as we know it depends decisively on the extent to which the church is able to participate in this transformation itself, trying to set appropriate accents which ensure that the religious dimension will be preserved in future for all cultural life. If the church pays close attention to the communicative possibilities of the internet for this purpose, then that will involve a fundamental change in the communication structure of churches and parishes.

This is not least due to the fact that in the social media communicative relevance depends on whether and to what extent the partners in a network are willing and able to maintain contact with the other participants or the community as a whole. On the one hand, social media rely heavily on personalised communication, and on the other hand they are interested in individuals being able to integrate into the group. Communication in the network is on an equal footing, is in principle polyphonic and can prove to be distinctly controversial. It is decisive that normally the respective status or position in the group plays no role for the communication. This is where social media differ completely from the structures commonly used when communicating via church media. It is important to be aware of this and to think carefully about where and how the church makes use of the social media. The opportunities they open up for further democratisation of the communication structures of the church and the parishes should certainly not remain unused.

14. Free – and free of charge

As is the case for other areas of society, religion can only function practically by means of structural organisations such as churches and parishes. They are in a position to establish permanent patterns of interpretation and action and to cater to religious motifs and motivations, so that they represent modern institutions of religious practice. However, this does not mean that the actions of the church are identical with religious practice. Nevertheless, the close-knit religious communication processes organised in the local churches allow religious themes, contexts and traditions to be continually repeated, ritualised and institutionalised.

However, one must understand that human religion is in need of linguistic or symbolic models of interpretation of the Christian faith which are offered and conveyed by the church, but does not simply recognize and accept such models. Rather, individual faith arises by adapting these models on the basis of one's own interpretations, which may well differ substantially from the interpretations given by the church. It is of great importance that personal faith emerges by self-determined appropriation. For this reason, the local churches have to shape their communicative approaches to religious contents in such a way that they may be dealt with individually and adapted to individual needs – even if this means that people do not reduce their distance from the church. But that is exactly what corresponds to an understanding which does not see the church as an association which regularly brings all its members together physically and visibly, but rather as an institution which leaves it up to each individual to decide whether and when he/she will make use of it. The ideal church would provide a basis on which to stand and would respect the autonomy a person has gained; such a church would never insist on excessive engagement and frenzied activity, but would be there when needed.

Such a church offers the stage for an encounter with the transcendental dimension of life and thus creates space for the spirit – but it is also seriously aware that it is not in its power to determine whether this spirit is felt or this encounter really happens. This church tells extraordinary stories – because it lives on the truth. It blesses all who come to it – irrespective of the person. It gives support and attention, offers help with symbolic language and religious rites – all without payment, free of charge. It does care for itself, but only for its mission. It reckons with God and always reminds (itself) that he is greater than the church. As a result, it also reckons with the fact that the truth is not only to be found in and through the church. It derives its credibility from justification by faith alone. It knows that God's grace is sufficient – and thus symbolises the anticipation of a new world to come.

Bernd Oberdorfer

Fellowship in Practice

Ecumenism from a Lutheran Perspective

1. Introduction

Ecumenism: global fellowship on the road

The anniversary of the Reformation in 2017 was purposely celebrated ecumenically. The Protestant churches did not wish to use the recollection of the events that led to the Reformation 500 years ago to distinguish themselves from other denominations, but wanted to emphasize what they had in common despite all diversity. The guiding principle was: »There is more connecting than dividing us.«

A Lutheran-Roman Catholic report was given the meaningful title »From Conflict to Communion«. On this basis, leading representatives of the Lutheran World Federation (LWF), including President Munib Younan and General Secretary Martin Junge, and the Roman Catholic Church, including Pope Francis, were able to ring in the commemoration year at a joint service of worship on Reformation Day 2016 in Lund, Sweden. On the same day in Malmö, they also agreed to cooperate closely in their social and charitable service to the world.

The Reformation anniversary was also consciously commemorated as a global event. For although the Reformation had its origins in the German-speaking world, its effects already reached far beyond those boundaries in the sixteenth century. The Reformation is now in the words of Martin Junge a »global citizen«. Nowadays, Protestant churches also consider themselves to be world churches and are organised in global associations, cultivating their relationships on a variety of different levels. In this sense, they also see themselves as ecumenical bodies.

Both these dimensions are crucial to the concept of ecumenism. The word originally means »the inhabited earth«, thus denoting the wide-ranging horizon of commonality in human culture. With reference to Christianity, it simply describes the cross-cultural extent of the command to proclaim the gospel to all nations. This goes hand in hand with the intention of articulating the inner connections between all regional churches. In this regard, »ecumenical« means the same as »catholic«. Christian communities do not exist in isolation from each other, but form »one body« spiritually.

Spiritual unity seeks visible expression. From the very outset, Christianity faced the challenge of discovering the ties within its diversity and of finding a form which would not contradict such diversity. At the same time, it was a question of defining the boundaries of diversity; this led inevitably to the expulsion of groups and attitudes which were qualified as heretical. It was repeatedly necessary to clarify this question: where and how is the true church visible? After centuries of mutual denunciation, the ecumenical movement of the twentieth century provided the answer with the emphatic confession: it is no longer merely visible in one's own denomination!

The first section of this short book sketches out a few historical developments to show how the relationship between diversity and the cultivation of connectedness has been realised in many diverse ways during the course of Christian history. The second chapter outlines the new approach of the ecumenical movement in the twentieth century. A central element was the search for theological doctrinal agreement; the most important results are presented in the third chapter from a Lutheran perspective. Further sections deal with the basic issues of ecumenism. The fourth chapter goes into more detail in clarifying what ecumenism is. Chapters five and six discuss denominational perspectives on church unity as well as ecumenical models and targets. Part seven goes into important dimensions for the cultivation of ecumenical connectedness. At the end, there is a forecast on the sustainability of the ecumenical awakening.

2. Unity and diversity – a historical overview

It was clear from the outset that the spiritual bonds between the Christian communities had to be visible. But no binding structures existed to achieve that. It was rather the case that different forms developed during the early centuries of Christianity which affirmed the fellowship and fostered relationships. None of these forms was generally recognised as alone decisive; and there was certainly no question of rigid organisational unity.

At a very early stage, the collection for the church in Jerusalem which Paul instigated on his missionary journeys demonstrates the awareness of responsibility for the whole of Christianity: »If one member suffers, all suffer together with it« (1 Cor 12:26). One major factor for the formation of a Christian identity was the selection and collection of early Christian writings into a canon, which then attained generally binding validity as the New Testament together with the Hebrew Bible, now known as the Old Testament. It is indeed astonishing to see what a wide range of highly differing theological thinking was included in this canon without apparently being seen as a threat to the Christian fellowship; incidentally, down to the present day no universal agreement on the arrangement and selection of texts in the Christian Bible has managed to prevail.

In order to achieve consciousness for the bonds between Christians, it was also of the utmost importance to formulate concise summaries of the principal elements of their belief in »rules of faith« (*regulae fidei*). These then led to creeds which served as orientation for the faith life of the Christian community. In the longer term, it was only the so-called Niceno-Constantinopolitan Creed which gained overall validity (the Apostolic Creed is only used in the Western churches). However, a (still not entirely resolved) dispute about the wording of the Creed, the so-called »Filioque controversy«, broke out between the Western and the Eastern Church. The Latin text, other than the original Greek version, added that the Holy Spirit proceeded from the Father »and the Son« (Latin: *filioque*), which was never accepted in Orthodoxy. This reduced the integrative effect of the Creed considerably.

Finally, it is necessary to mention the formation of authoritative leadership structures, particularly the episcopal ministry, which initially fulfilled the function of symbolising and stabilising the unity of the local church. Given that the authority of the bishops was traced back to the apostles, it was only a short step to see the gathering of bishops as an image of the gathering of the apostles. Down to the present day, the Orthodox and Catholic traditions, as well as the Anglican churches, preserve this tradition.

When the state persecution of Christians came to an end and Christianity was officially promoted by Constantine the Great, the unity of the Church as imperial church gained important significance for the Roman state. The first Council of Bishops on an imperial level, later known as the (First) Ecumenical Council of Nicea, was convened in 325 by Constantine himself; he had an interest in ensuring that the vehement theological disputes between Christians concerning the relationship of Christ (and the Holy Spirit) to God should be overcome by a consensus. The success proved to be short-lived at best. Nonetheless, the model of an ecumenical Council was continued; the dispute was ended at the Second Council in Constantinople in 381, which declared the Trinitarian understanding of God to be a binding dogma. This was followed by a Christological controversy over the relationship between divinity and humanity in the person of Jesus Christ, which lasted decades and was finally resolved in 451 at the Council of Chalcedon. Nonetheless, the doctrine of the two natures did not meet with general acceptance, so that unity could not be preserved; the Chalcedonian churches (principally Greek Orthodox and Latin Catholic) and the non-Chalcedonian churches (Oriental Orthodox, formerly known as Monophysites) went separate ways and still do so today. The Ecumenical Council was *de facto* no longer representative of ecumenical Christianity.

Nevertheless, it can be said that the Councils formed an overarching link between the Christians in the Greek-speaking East and the Latin-speaking West of the Roman Empire. One feature was the idea of the Pentarchy, according to which the five patriarchates of Rome, Constantinople, Alexandria, Jerusalem and Antioch represented jointly the entire Christian world. After the fall of the Western Roman Empire (476), whereby Western Christianity passed into the Germanic-Gothic cultural area, Western and Eastern Christianity gradually drifted apart. The Roman popes' increasing claim to represent the one universal Church in their own person only developed an integrative force in the West; it encountered massive rejection in the East, thus reinforcing the tendencies to divergence. The mutual excommunication of the Pope and the Patriarch in Constantinople in 1054 was only seen much later retrospectively as the symbolic date of the East-West Schism; but the separation was sealed at the latest in 1204 when Western Crusaders conquered and looted Constantinople, an act perceived by the Greeks as outrageous humiliation of Christians by Christians. The so-called Union Councils of Lyon (1274) and especially Ferrara-Florence (1438–1443) are proof of the continuing sense of (ecumenical) Christian unity; however, these efforts remained unsuccessful.

With the developments in the Reformation period, the process of differentiation was further accelerated. The Reformation was originally intended to be a reform movement within the one Church. But when the reform demands and their underlying understanding of the gospel were rejected by the Roman Church as heretical, the Reformers saw themselves compelled to build their own church structures. Significant differences of opinion also came to light within the reform movement. In particular, different understandings on the Lord's Supper led to the formation of separate Lutheran and Reformed (or Calvinist) churches that were not in ecclesial communion with one another. Both of them, as well as the Roman Catholics, opposed the Anabaptist groups, who founded their own church traditions. After the separation of the English Church from Rome, an Anglican type emerged which remained connected with the Roman model liturgically and in its respect for the episcopate, but took over strong reformatory impulses theologically. At the Council of Trent (Tridentinum, 1545–1563) the Roman Catholic Church was re-organised and clearly dissociated from the Reformation forces, thus effectively becoming one denominational church among others.

Over the course of the succeeding centuries, religious diversity increased and became more and more established. Movements for inner-Protestant renewal developed into new churches such as the Methodists and the Moravian Church. Groups that had been driven out of Europe, for example the Baptists or the Mennonites, formed independent church communities, especially in North America, which were later re-imported into Europe, as it were. The Quakers or the Salvation Army formed special kinds of Christian groups. In 1870, the dispute over the dogma of the infallibility of the pope led to a split within the Tridentine tradition between the Roman Catholic and the Old Catholic Church. In the twentieth century, the Pentecostal movement developed out of the Baptist tradition and is now correctly regarded as an independent, fourth denominational family alongside Orthodoxy, Catholicism and Protestantism. Christianity has never been as diverse as it is today.

Nevertheless, the awareness that Christendom is fundamentally united has never been quite lost and has repeatedly unleashed renewed attempts to reach interdenominational agreements. In particular, during the first decades of the Reformation, Melanchthon promoted colloquies intended to overcome the differences with the Roman Church. Although they drew nearer to one another thematically, the conversations brought no practical consequences. Melanchthon also tried to get into contact with Orthodoxy, and suggested among other things that the Augsburg Confession be translated into Greek. Later, there was a lengthy correspondence between Lutheran theologians in Tübingen and Patriarch Jeremias II of Constantinople; but it was broken off when the differences proved to be too serious.

In the seventeenth century, the destructive power of denominational claims to exclusivity was made evident by armed conflicts, including some lengthy wars. The Peace of Westphalia of 1648 secured denominational diversity in the long term. In the wake of this treaty, the persecution and expulsion of the Protestant Huguenots in France after 1685 was already an anachronism. At the same time, dogmatic differences were relativized by Pietism, which emphasised the devotion of the heart, and by the Enlightenment with its emphasis on reason. Within Protestantism, doctrinal differences between Calvinism and Lutheranism were increasingly perceived as not church-dividing. Therefore, in the nineteenth century United Protestant churches came into being in Germany, which indeed provoked strong opposition and resistance, particularly on the part of the Lutherans.

However, the strengthening consciousness of the bonds between Protestants was accompanied by a sharper dissociation from Catholicism. In the seventeenth century, the Lutheran theologian Georg Calixtus had already proposed that the dogmatic consensus of the first five Christian centuries (*consensus quinquesaecularis*) should form the basis of an understanding with Rome (and Byzantium), and the Lutheran-minded philosopher Gottfried Wilhelm Leibniz had sought dialogue with Catholic theologians by means of religiously open reason. Pietists such as August Hermann Francke also drew inspiration from Catholic mystic piety; Nikolaus Ludwig von Zinzendorf even respected the denominations in a positive sense as God's various »paths to education«, none of which could claim to be exclusively right. In the longer term, Protestantism distinguished itself, nevertheless, increasingly as a modern counterpart to the Roman church, which was considered to be authoritarian in dogma and traditionalist. In the other direction, the Roman Catholic Church now emphasised its unique position in the Christian world more strongly, focussed its hierarchical self-understanding radically on the papacy and emphatically rejected the cultural and social developments of the modern age (»anti-modernism«).

In contrast, the Old Catholic Church sought agreement with the Anglican and Orthodox churches from the outset. In this way, it was to some extent the forerunner of the twentieth century ecumenical movement.

3. The ecumenical movement

The ecumenical movement is undoubtedly an outstanding event in modern Christian history. The twentieth century has rightly been denoted the »century of ecumenism«. How did this movement come about? Several factors should be mentioned:

First of all, as a consequence of worldwide mission, which experienced an enormous surge in the nineteenth century, it became clear that competition between denominations which mutually discredited one another did significant damage to the credibility of the Christian message; this endangered the further spread of the gospel. It was not by chance that the ecumenical movement materialised for the first time at the World Missionary Conference in Edinburgh (1910). Mission was addressed there as a common challenge for all churches and it was agreed that cooperation in this field be strengthened. There was also increasing awareness for the churches' common responsibility for witness by action and service to the world – especially in view of the suffering endured in the Great War. For this reason the »Life and Work« Commission was one of the first institutionalised forms of ecumenism. At the same time it became increasingly clear that long-term ecumenical understanding could not exist without tackling disputed theological questions. Therefore the »Faith and Order« Commission first convened in 1927 in order to identify in multilateral theological reflection the separating and the unifying factors and to deepen ecclesial fellowship theologically.

These first attempts were dominated by the Protestants. It is all the more remarkable that Orthodoxy very soon took an active part in the ecumenical movement. In 1920 the Patriarch of Constantinople called upon the churches in an official statement to make efforts towards Christian unity.

Thanks to these and other initiatives, which enriched one another mutually, inter-denominational networks and inter-regional ecumenical relationships emerged in the period between the two world wars. Personal meetings also created trustworthy friendships across confessional and cultural boundaries, which proved their worth even in the ideologically charged, aggressive international conflicts of the Second World War. The horrifying experiences of this World War also made it clear that the Christian churches had to take up responsibility for reconciliation, peace and justice in the world, which they could only achieve jointly. It is therefore no coincidence that important ecumenical institutions formed immediately after the war.

Special mention should be made here of the World Council of Churches (WCC), founded in Amsterdam in 1948 (after first attempts during the interwar period). It brought together the initiatives already referred to in the fields of missionary activity, world service and theological understanding and saw itself programmatically as the broadest possible forum of Christian churches with the aim of deepening their fellowship and unifying their witness for and in the world. This purpose is served above all at the regular Assemblies, held every six to seven years (most recently in 2013 in Busan, South Korea). After initial hesitation, most of the Orthodox churches joined the WCC as members, although they continue to express their reservations repeatedly against what they see as Protestant domination of the Council. In the wake of some intense controversies (women's ordination; homosexuality) some of them even chose to leave the WCC.

At first, the Roman Catholic Church officially kept its distance from the ecumenical movement, being unable to see itself dogmatically as one church among several Christian churches and understanding ecumenism primarily in the sense of reuniting the »renegade« Christians and Christian groups under its own roof. Informally however, Roman Catholic clergy and lay people took an intensive interest in the ecumenical movement from the outset. The Second Vatican Council (1962–1965) marked an important turning point: in its document »*Unitatis Redintegratio*« the Catholic Church welcomed the ecumenical movement explicitly as a promising »sign of the times« and acknowledged that beyond its own boundaries there was not just sporadic Christian witness, but also respectable forms of church life and fellowship. At the latest since then, the Catholic Church commits itself officially to participation in ecumenical dialogues, preferably on a global level with the denominational bodies which also were formed after the Second World War.

In 1947 in Lund, Sweden, Lutheran churches from all over the world joined together to form the Lutheran World Federation (LWF). In the world situation after World War II, they determined to dedicate themselves to active solidarity in reconstruction and renewal in the face of all the devastation and the suffering of so many people. The LWF also saw the need for spiritual reconciliation. It consciously gave itself the form of a federation, meaning an association of churches that remained independent. There was no intention of creating a »Lutheran Vatican«. However, in view of the growing awareness of the ties between its members, the LWF defined itself explicitly in 1990 as a communion of churches in the sense of full pulpit and altar fellowship and made a corresponding addition to its name.

Other Protestant denominations such as the Reformed, Methodist and Mennonite churches strengthened their worldwide organisational networks as well. The Anglican churches which had been founded in the countries of the British Empire constituted their global community in spite of the fact that the political ties had been abolished. These developments reflect the global spread of Christianity that has taken place within the respective confessional families, and they demonstrate an elementary shift: former mission fields have been replaced by independent churches which now stand alongside their former mother churches as partners on an equal footing.

The close-knit relationship between the denominations was also to be observed on the national level. In many countries, national Councils of Churches were founded, for example in 1948 the »Council of Churches in Germany« (ACK), which seeks to fulfil its statutory task of promoting »the common witness and service« of the member churches by means of a variety of activities (Week of Prayer for Christian Unity, Ecumenical Day of Prayer for the Care of Creation, etc.). Its German Ecumenical Studies Committee (DÖSTA) also contributes to multi-denominational theological reflection.

4. The search for doctrinal consensus

The ecumenical movement derived its dynamics from the various experiences connecting the life-world of Christians from different confessional backgrounds. This led to the question whether there might not be so much common ground to be found within the various forms of Christian practice that the traditional one-sided or mutual condemnations pronounced by different churches concerning doctrine, leadership structures or forms of worship could be overcome. The aim of the resulting ecumenical doctrinal dialogues was not the elimination of differences, but the unanimous recognition that such differences are not, or are no longer, church-dividing and do not form a hindrance to ecclesial communion.

The task was twofold: on the one hand, the question was whether the teaching of the churches involved had in the meantime, since the separation, changed to such an extent that the condemnations of that time no longer corresponded to the present-day doctrine held by the respective church. On the other hand, in the light of the accordance reached today, it was necessary to see whether the historical doctrinal condemnations were not even at the time unjustified in respect to the teaching of the church being criticised, had it been correctly understood, although this had been perceived differently by the contemporaries (on both sides).

It is impossible even to provide a short summary of the results of the various ecumenical doctrinal dialogues here; the collection of »Documents of Growing Accordance« (German: »Dokumente wachsender Übereinstimmung«) fills four bulky volumes. From a Lutheran perspective, these are the most significant dialogues:

A milestone within the ecumenism of Protestant churches is the Leuenberg Agreement. On the basis of a fundamental agreement in the understanding of the gospel and the sacraments, Lutheran, Reformed and United churches in Europe declared in 1973 that the doctrinal differences that had existed since the Reformation (especially in the understanding of the Lord's Supper) no longer needed to lead to divisions between the churches, and they expressed their full church communion, i.e. pulpit and altar communion. The deepening of this communion, which had already been proposed within the Agreement, was put into practice with the foundation of the Community of Protestant Churches in Europe (CPCE).

In 1967, shortly after the Second Vatican Council, an official theological dialogue between the LWF and the Roman Catholic Church was started on a global level and has continued since then without interruption. The outstanding result was the »Joint Declaration on the Doctrine of Justification« (JDDJ), which was signed after a lengthy process of genesis and reception on 31 October 1999 in Augsburg. Both churches saw a »consensus in basic truths« with regard to the doctrine of justification, which had been the cause of particular controversy at the Reformation period, and in the light of this consensus they judged the remaining differences to be indeed serious, but no longer church-dividing. However, since other church-dividing differences, notably in the understanding of the ordained ministry, were not repealed by this document, the JDDJ had no direct practical consequences; Lutherans remained excluded from the Catholic Eucharist. Nonetheless, the consensus proved to be so viable theologically that it was subsequently also adopted by the worldwide fellowships of Methodist (2006) and Reformed (2017) churches, while the Anglican Communion also signaled approval in 2017. The JDDJ also exercised an influence by creating a lasting confidence-building effect. This was demonstrated by the fact that it was possible to mark the Reformation anniversary – as mentioned – with a joint commemoration.

With the Anglican Communion, the understanding of the episcopal ministry proved to be the only difference which stood in the way of full ecclesial communion. In this case the dialogues were conducted not only at the global level, but also in various regions. Here different historically determined accents within Lutheranism became noticeable. While the episcopal tradition was discontinued in Germany in the sixteenth century and only resumed with alterations in the twentieth century, the Scandinavian Lutherans have an unbroken relationship to the episcopate, both historically and factually. Therefore, they were able to agree upon full communion with the Anglican Churches of England, Wales, Scotland and Ireland in Porvoo in 1992. The equivalent is also the case in North America. Although this stage has not yet been reached in Germany, the Meissen Agreement of 1988 between the EKD and the Church of England was able to achieve far-reaching consensus, thus enabling Eucharistic fellowship.

From their beginnings, the Old Catholics understood themselves to be very close to the Anglicans theologically. Moreover, they also opened themselves increasingly to Reformation influences, for example on the issue of women's ordination. In Germany mutual Eucharistic hospitality was agreed in 1985 between the EKD and the Old Catholic Church. As with the Anglicans, the Lutheran dialogue with the Old Catholics focused on the understanding of the episcopal ministry. The aim is full ecclesial communion, although this has not yet been achieved; important steps such as the mutual recognition of Confirmation and the development of a common ecumenical marriage ceremony have already been taken.

On the basis of general theological convergence, the Lutheran-Baptist dialogue was able to take a fresh look at the particularly controversial issue of infant baptism and believer's or adult baptism. In the regional dialogue of a Bavarian Baptist-Lutheran working group (BALUBAG) the following idea that was common to both sides was emphasized: baptism is part of an initiation process leading into the Christian life, whereby for the Lutherans it takes place at the beginning of the road, and for the Baptists at the end. The working group saw this insight as a basis for full ecclesial communion. Misgivings on this conclusion were raised in both churches, whilst there was certainly recognition that progress had been made in the matter; it is indisputable that one is now closer to agreement than in the sixteenth century. BALUBAG's results at least led to the start of official doctrinal discussions between the VELKD and the Baptist Union of Evangelical Free Churches (BEFG) on a national level at the end of 2017, with the aim of achieving the most far-reaching ecclesial communion possible.

The dialogue with the Mennonites was conducted on a different level. Since the recollection of their persecution in the sixteenth century continued to weigh heavily for the Mennonites on their relationship to the Lutherans, it was necessary first of all to tackle the historical events jointly. In this way mutual trust increased, finally resulting in an act of reconciliation at the LWF Assembly in Stuttgart in 2010, in which the Lutherans asked the Mennonites for forgiveness for the persecution in the past. This »healing of memories« created room for discussion on theological differences.

The dialogue with the Orthodox Churches has a unique character. It has been held continuously for many decades both in Germany as well as on a global level. The aim lies less on the production of official consensus documents than on mutual confidence building. Even if there are practically no tangible results, that does not signify ineffectiveness; to a certain extent it is true that in this case the path – meaning the maintenance of the dialogue – is indeed already the goal.

Special attention should be paid to multilateral dialogues involving several churches and ideally a wide range. One example of this is the so-called Lima paper »Baptism, Eucharist and Ministry«, which led to a great deal of discussion and also criticism. With this document the Faith and Order Commission of the WCC tried in 1982 to formulate »convergences« in the different confessional traditions concerning the central topics of church doctrine and practice named in the title. The »Lima Liturgy«, which was developed on this basis, also had a strong impact.

The ecumenical dialogues were fostered and accompanied by the reflection in academic theology. Institutions such as the

Institute for Ecumenical Research in Strasbourg (which is closely related to the LWF) or the Catholic Johann-Adam-Möhler Institute in Paderborn provided important impulses. Some theological faculties also founded chairs of Ecumenical Theology. Textbooks for Ecumenical Dogmatics (e.g. Schlink 1984, Bienert/Kühn 2013) signalled openness at the very heart of denominational self-understanding.

Ecumenical doctrinal dialogues aimed at reaching a theological consensus or on identifying or deepening an existing consensus, do not take place in a vacuum. They presuppose a basic awareness of the commonality between the participating churches and their members, and this awareness spawns the intimation that differences in doctrine (meaning the understanding of the essential contents of the Christian faith) are not so crucial as to prevent church fellowship (or a greater level of church fellowship). Doctrinal consensus does not generate fellowship, but gives it significant expression and may well promote it. However, they are neither the only expression of fellowship, nor the prerequisite for it. On the contrary, they are often the result of fellowship which is already being practised. Retrospectively, they catch up with the development on a theoretical level, stabilise and strengthen it. Conversely, doctrinal agreements make no sense and literally lose their »setting in life« if there is no equivalent in the real life of the churches concerned.

What kind of fellowship is meant by the expression »ecumenism«? What is its aim? This leads to fundamental questions of ecumenical theology which will now be discussed from a Lutheran point of view.

5. What is ecumenism?

Ecumenism is the cultivation of connections. It is based on an awareness that there are ties connecting all Christians and that these are worth caring for and need to be maintained.

This may sound obvious, but it is not so in the least. It is indeed generally accepted in the whole of Christendom that there is only one church of Jesus Christ, just as – and therefore because – there is only one Christ. All Christians are connected as members of the one body of Christ. Broad consensus also exists that the church does not just have a spiritual and intellectual dimension, but also needs to have visible and concrete forms and practices.

For a very long time, the factual variety of such visible forms was dealt with by resorting to the concepts of true and false religions or churches: one's own church is considered to be the one and only legitimate form representing the true church. Other forms are condemned as heterodox or heretical; their claim to be a church is thus disputed. Everything outside the light counts as shadow. These mechanisms of mutual exclusion became particularly obvious during the century of the Reformation. The Roman Church saw the Reformation as heresy and renounced it by excommunicating Luther and by pronouncing condemnations (*anathema sit* – »be rejected«) at the Council of Trent. For their part, the Reformers judged that their oppression and persecution had proved the Roman church to be false (and thus even a diabolical instrument of the Antichrist). The Peace of Augsburg of 1555 was therefore not a religious but a political peace, ultimately forced upon both sides against their will. It secured a coexistence in which the two churches agreed to differ peacefully, whilst mutually refusing to accept the other side as a true church. There could be no question of ecumenism in the modern sense.

The fact that this changed fundamentally is historically due to a fundamental shift of consciousness which became tangible around the beginning of the twentieth century after a number of previous attempts. Even today it is possible to sense the feeling of euphoria aroused by the discovery that there were authentic Christians, even authentic churches, beyond the bounds of one's own denomination. Differing types of Christian existence were now primarily perceived as an opportunity to enrich one's own Christian experience, and not as a heresy which had to be vanquished. This unleashed dynamic forces seeking to identify and extend commonalities on a variety of different levels. They ranged from loose forms of mutual esteem and combined actions of social care to joint prayer and worship meetings, even to church services with closer forms of hospitality and fellowship. The momentum extended from academic conferences to discussions on doctrinal consensus, formal mutual recognition and church communion and even organisational unification.

It is possible to identify a whole range of factors which initiated and encourages this development, such as these:

- Social and cultural modernisation affects all denominations (or their members) and reduces their cultural differences in the worldly environment.
- Common challenges (e.g. atheism, totalitarianism) accentuate the consciousness of common Christian responsibility.
- Increasing mobility changes the previously homogeneous denominational milieu, leading to a mixed population and manifold contacts between the denominations; this may be

observed for example in the growing number of interdenominational marriages and families, which no longer have to fear a limited social acceptance nowadays.

- In this connection, there is a better knowledge and understanding of the cultures of piety and devotional rites in other Christian traditions, so that these are recognised – regardless of all differences – as socially plausible, at least subjectively authentic expressions of the common Christian faith.
- In the face of a multitude of meetings and experiences of general Christian, interdenominational fellowship, doctrinal differences dwindle or lose their significance for the practice of faith.
- Spiritual movements that ignore denominational boundaries – such as the liturgical movement, the charismatic renewal, or individual groups like Taizé – put interdenominational styles of life and piety into exemplary practice.
- The globalisation of Christianity means that Christians in the former mission fields do not identify so strongly with their denominations as is the case in the churches which sent out missionaries and had developed a strong confessional profile in the course of history.

As a result of these developments, exclusivist claims by individual denominations to sole representation have become questionable and a consciousness of a general fellowship between all Christians has grown. However, it is wrong to assume that the diversity of denominational backgrounds and traditions now has to be understood as a fundamental deficiency that must be overcome. Nonetheless, very different ideas have evolved with respect to the ways in which this interdenominational fellowship awareness should be, or even must be, articulated. Is it sufficient, for example, to declare officially that church services or Holy Communion are reciprocally opened to members of other denominations (Eucharistic hospitality)? Or is it necessary to instate a stronger institutional form for the elementary Christian unity attested in the Creed and »felt« in this ecumenical fellowship awareness? And if so, what degree of institutionalisation is required? Are there elements of institutional structure which are mandatory for the visible unity of the Church?

6. Denominational perspectives on church unity

It is no wonder that denominational differences reassert themselves when answering these questions. For the Roman Catholic Church it is clear that the unity of the Church must have a binding organisational form. This primarily includes the episcopate in the succession of the Apostles; within the communion of bishops, the Pope as Bishop of Rome is entrusted with a special unifying function. Full ecclesial communion is only possible where this binding structure is fully recognised. For the Anglican, Old Catholic and Orthodox churches the episcopal ministry and the communion of bishops are also the necessary expression of their apostolic origin and comprehensive ecclesial communion. But they reject the idea that, in addition to that, a papacy endowed with ultimately binding authority is necessary for the unity of the Church. At the other end of the spectrum, there are churches from the Anabaptist tradition, such as Baptists or Mennonites, who see the unity of the church implemented in a local context, and therefore have only developed loose regional or national networks.

From this point of view, it is not necessary to strive for stronger structural homogeneity of denominations; ecumenical ties express themselves in mutual recognition and ecclesial hospitality.

Where does the Lutheran Church stand? Lutheran tradition takes it for granted that there is only one church of Jesus Christ. The Reformers did not originally want to form their own church, but to reform the existing church. The being of the church is defined by content. The famous seventh article of the Augsburg Confession of 1530 describes the church as a »gathering of all believers, among whom the gospel is purely preached and the holy sacraments are administered in accordance with the gospel«. This confession identifies the church on the basis of preaching and the sacraments as the central means for communicating the gospel. Church is where the gospel comes into effect »purely« in word and sacrament.

Based on this fundamental definition, the Confession now infers conditions for the »true [...] unity of the Christian church«. It is »sufficient« if in the different congregations »the gospel is preached there in harmony according to a pure understanding of it and the sacraments are administered there according to God's Word«. Wherever there is such consensus in the understanding of the gospel and the administration of the sacraments, it is »not necessary that traditions [literally »ceremonies«] instituted by men should be everywhere alike«. (CA 7) So there might be differences in the orders and practices of the church that do not compromise the ecclesial communion. These include the clerical vestments; the order and form of liturgy at worship services; organisational structure; designation and function of leadership bodies, etc. According to Lutheran understanding, the proper communication of the gospel essentially requires a special ministry of public proclamation of the gospel and administration of the sacraments, for which a »regular call« (cf. CA 14) is necessary. However, the specific way in which this calling takes place is not laid down in the gospel itself and is therefore variable. This principle also applies to supra-congregational leadership responsibility (episkopé). For this reason the Reformers did not reject the ministry of the bishops, but they did not consider it to be an essential factor for the church's existence as such; supra-regional church leadership is indeed necessary, but it can be achieved with other institutional forms.

This distinction between the necessary consensus in the understanding of the gospel and the formal diversity of human traditions in theology and church life ensure that Lutheranism is in principle open to the recognition of other churches as legitimate forms of expression of the Christian faith and to full ecclesial communion with them. However, from a Lutheran perspective there is no binding model for the structure of such ecclesial communion. Given a basic agreement on the content of the faith, church unity can be realised as a communion of organisationally separate churches with different liturgies, leadership structures or theology. This is the model followed by the Leuenberg Agreement. Unity can also take the form of an organisational association, as is demonstrated by the unions between Lutheran and Reformed churches in Germany in the nineteenth century which still exist today in the member churches of the Union of Evangelical Churches (UEK) within the EKD. But the history of these unions also shows that denominational differences often persist within the United Churches. In addition, there have repeatedly been Lutherans who refused to enter such associations, even preferring in some cases to emigrate rather than to adapt to the changed conditions. Factually, the unions have therefore increased the denominational diversity in German Protestantism, rather than diminishing it.

While Lutheranism traditionally paid little attention to developing forms of supra-regional coordination and leadership responsibility, there appears to be a growing awareness at present that church fellowship extending beyond individual parishes or regional churches needs visible forms of expression and institutional frameworks. One proof of this within the Lutheran confessional family at the German level is provided by the founding of the United Evangelical Lutheran Church of Germany (VELKD), to which almost all Lutheran churches belong as members, as well as the international Lutheran World Federation (LWF), which came into existence at almost the same time and currently numbers 148 Lutheran member churches from 99 countries. Lutheran churches are actively engaged interdenominationally in the Community of Protestant Churches in Europe (CPCE) or extensively in the World Council of Churches (WCC). In bilateral dialogue with other denominations they seek to issue joint statements reliably documenting the degree of ecclesial communion achieved.

These supra-regional structures differ in the extent of their formal authority. None of them comes even close to the level of obligation ascribed by the Roman Catholic Church to the communion of bishops with the Pope at the centre. In principle, by the way, Lutheran ecclesiology by no means excludes an office representing the unity of the world church. For example, in the sense of a »human tradition« as quoted in CA 7, Melanchthon was prepared to recognise the papacy for the sake of unity and peace in Christendom as a symbol and authority for the preservation of that unity. Luther was able to agree in principle, but saw it as a practical dilemma that a religiously based papal authority could not be deduced from the gospel. A »merely« human legitimacy for the papacy would on the other hand not be sufficient to command the loyalty of the faithful, and would therefore not serve the purpose of ensuring unity. This argument has not lost its relevance. From a Lutheran point of view it is quite reasonable to think about personal forms to represent and bear responsibility for the ecumenical unity of the world-wide church. But it is neither theologically nor pragmatically necessary to call on the papacy as the only approach to this end. The term »Petrine ministry« is a popular but unfortunate expression for this function, since it immediately restricts the possibilities to this office. In addition, a representative of church unity would also have primarily symbolic significance; the institution of a higher-ranking central authority endued with strong powers over the individual churches, or even with the right to bring disciplinary measures against them, would hardly have a chance of being accepted by Protestants.

7. Ecumenical models for the unity of the church

From the beginning, the ecumenical movement was concerned with the question of the aim to be achieved by interdenominational understanding. Was it organisational union of the previously separate churches? Or is unity complete if the diversity of the churches is retained while they overcome their differences, recognise each other unreservedly as valid forms of the one church of Jesus Christ and live in full communion in every respect despite organisational autonomy? The latter is the model underlying the Leuenberg Agreement. The former is the preference of the Roman Catholic Church, which does not regard the unity of the church as sufficiently articulated and maintained in a juxtaposition of mutually recognised denominations.

It is important to note that nowadays no conception of church unity aims to let the diversity of denominational characteristics vanish in one unified church. Even the Roman Catholic Church does not pursue »retro-ecumenism« in the sense that the other denominations should abandon their respective traditions, admitting that they were aberrations. It emphasises its appreciation of these traditions, which could be upheld within the Roman Catholic Church, and can also refer to models in which the union with Rome is compatible with a high degree of continuing independence, for example in matters of liturgy and church order, as is the case with the Oriental Catholic or Uniate churches. Nonetheless, for the Roman Catholic Church, the organisational reintegration, meaning the recognition of the episcopal and papal order, is the necessary condition for full ecclesial communion, without which joint celebrations of Holy Communion or even Eucharistic hospitality are impossible.

Conversely, the model of unity in diversity is not satisfied with a loose arrangement of denominational churches existing side by side with little interest in ecumenical fellowship. It is no coincidence that the Leuenberg Agreement called on the churches involved to deepen their fellowship through further discussions based on the theological convergences achieved. The outcome was the founding of the Community of Protestant Churches in Europe (CPCE).

Against this background, expressions such as »visible unity« or »unity in reconciled diversity« have the advantage that they hold on to the necessity of a visible bond between all Christians, whose form includes the institutional church dimension, without determining in advance the concrete implementation of this unity. But this is at the same time a disadvantage of such expressions. They are ambiguous and therefore open to manifold interpretations of content. Thus talk of »unity in reconciled diversity« makes it clear that the unity being aimed at does not eliminate differences – it does not say »unity through«, but »unity in [...] diversity«. But clarification is still lacking as to what (institutional) consequences follow from the reconciliation of differences. This applies at least in the same measure to the »visible unity«. That is simply a rejection of an understanding of Christian unity which locates it behind and beyond denominational differentiation in an invisible spiritual communion that does not need to adopt an institutional form. It remains unsaid, however, which visible form unity should specifically adopt. Presumably, however, the meaning of such phrases consists in precisely this: holding on to the tasks in hand without prejudicing the solution.

8. Aspects of the cultivation of ecumenical connections

Ecumenism is the cultivation of connections. If the fundamental experience of the ecumenical movement is taken seriously, namely that the Christian faith is lived authentically in ecclesial forms beyond one's own denomination, this cannot fail to have consequences for the life of one's own specific church. If other churches are now also recognised as members of the body of Christ, then the words of the Apostle Paul that the rejoicing or the suffering of one member is shared by all the other members (1 Cor 12) also apply to the churches: they rejoice and suffer with one another in all that they do or feel. The existence of the churches is already cause for joy. Their spiritual traditions, especially in liturgy, theology and the practice of piety, as well as their culture-shaping charisma can be appreciated as an enrichment of one's own faith, instead of appearing to be a deviation from the truth.

This does not mean that things that are disconcerting, persistently strange or even false in the life and thinking of another church may no longer be identified as such. But this, too, must be done in a spirit of respect, which does not immediately disqualify whatever leads to irritation, but tries to understand its intention of giving authentic expression to the Christian faith. The controversy over truth is therefore not excluded; but it takes the form of a striving to teach and practise the gospel, in which brothers and sisters are willing to correct and instruct one another mutually.

By the same token, one church cannot disregard the other churches when shaping its own teaching and practice. The ecumenical community rather forms an essential horizon for the orientation of church teaching and life, which cannot be ignored. This does not mean that churches would be unable to make decisions unless consensus had been found with other churches (of their own and other denominational families); were that the case, Lutheran churches would still have not introduced the ordination of women into the ministry, for example. But it does mean that the views of ecumenical partners and the consequences of a decision for the ecumenical community should be taken into consideration during the decision-making process. Above all, however, it means accepting responsibility for the decisions taken in face of the ecumenical sister churches, communicating and expounding their theological justification in an open and understandable fashion. This may well take place in a spirit of inducement, harbouring the hope that other churches might be inspired by the decision of one church to take steps of their own; women's ordination can serve as a good example for this kind of ecumenical testimony. But precisely when it is to be expected that a decision will continue to arouse controversy ecumenically, there is a particularly strong challenge to implement and explain it in ecumenical responsibility.

The awareness of the ties within Christianity in general has come about through the experience of active fellowship and offers a strong impulse towards enabling new and common experiences of this kind. This takes place on many different levels and in various dimensions. These will be elucidated in the following sections. All of them are important. Well-known attempts to play off »bottom-up ecumenism« against »top-down ecumenism«, or »ecumenism of life« against »ecumenism of doctrine«, have proved to be of little help. Those bearing responsibility in the institutions of the established churches cannot be sweepingly characterised as over-cautious worriers who seek to thwart »top-down« the dynamic »bottom up« progress at the grass-roots; nor can one diminish the importance of finding interdenominational agreement in teaching (doctrinal consensus) in favour of concrete fellowship taking place in everyday life. It is nonetheless correct that ecumenical practice often represents a field for experimentation and learning, exploring new possibilities and extensions for fellowship and producing experiences that provide an impetus for theological reflection and adoption by the official church. The ecumenical movement would quickly have run out of steam without such creative spheres of ecumenical »civil disobedience« which did not wait for the churches to give official approval before going into action. However, it was often the theologians who demonstrated ingenuity, stringent conceptions and imagination as they sought to loosen or eradicate theological controversies that were deeply entrenched in ecclesiastical thinking. And it was not unusual for official church representatives to push interdenominational ties forward by gesture or decisions, thus encouraging their churches to take further steps (for example Pope Francis at his visit to Lund on Reformation Day 2016). In the longer term, the increased awareness for ecumenical fellowship will only prove to be sustainable if it is practised at all levels, that is to say, with lively contacts in parishes, solid reflection in theology and secure rulings in church order.

8.1 Worship fellowship

The primary expression of the bond between all Christians is the joint service of worship. The church life of every Christian denomination is founded and focussed on the celebration of services, each of them with specific forms. In this regard, ecumenism consists in the recognition and acknowledgment of constitutive elements of authentic Christian worship in the services held by other denominations, combined with the willingness to allow church members to participate in the services of other churches and to invite their members to worship in one's own church.

This is more demanding than it sounds. Indeed, there is no church that forbids members of other churches to attend its services as guests, and no church forbids its members to accept the hospitality of other churches at their worship. But the Roman Catholic Church requires its members to attend Roman Catholic Mass on Sunday and does not recognise Protestant services as an adequate equivalent to meet this »Sunday obligation«. The Orthodox churches even use the term »worship« exclusively for the »Divine Liturgy« which they celebrate. Nonetheless, both churches do not fundamentally deny that services in other churches have the quality of Christian devotions.

Ecumenical worship services that are jointly organised and celebrated go one step further. They are usually held in addition to the denominational services and mostly on special occasions (Week of Prayer for Christian Unity, World Day of Prayer; dedication of buildings; ecumenical parish festivities) or in a particular context (for example in a school or hospital). A special case is the church wedding ceremony for couples from different denominations, which is meanwhile known as »ecumenical marriage« although it is strictly speaking a Protestant ceremony with Catholic participation or vice versa; the ecumenical dimension is nevertheless unmistakable (and the Lutherans and Old Catholics have in fact already formulated a joint order for the marriage service which is ecumenical in the full sense of the word).

Joint ecumenical worship services or devotions are generally a particularly visible and effective expression of ecumenical ties. Admittedly, they take place outside the normal rhythm of worship in the respective denominations and develop specific liturgical forms, so that they are clearly recognisable as exceptions, thus drawing attention to the lasting differences between the confessions.

8.2 Eucharistic hospitality and altar fellowship

Holy Communion is a particularly sensory and intensive form of celebrating Christian fellowship. The sense of division therefore weighs all the heavier when congregations of different denominations cannot hold a service of communion together or when individual believers are excluded from participation in the communion service of another denomination. This is felt especially keenly by interdenominational couples.

The Protestant and Roman Catholic Churches agree that full ecclesial communion is the prerequisite for, and the consummate expression of, full inter-communion (Eucharistic fellowship); therefore, it is not yet possible between these churches. For several decades the Evangelical Church has invited baptised Christians of other confessions to participate in the Protestant communion service, because it does not feel entitled to exclude believers who trust in the presence of Christ at the Lord's Supper. It also points out that this experience of fellowship with other followers of Christ is an encouragement to take further steps. The Roman Catholic Church officially rejects such Eucharistic hospitality with exactly the opposite argument, saying that it leads to the false impression that full ecclesial communion already exists and thus counters the incentive to continue efforts in this direction. On the other hand, Lutheran churches have been able to agree on mutual Eucharistic hospitality with other churches such as the Anglicans and the Old Catholics, even though they are not yet in full communion with them. However, wherever full church communion has been achieved, as for example between Lutheran and Reformed churches, there is also full inter-communion in every respect; because these churches have mutually recognised the ordained ministry, joint communion celebrations are possible. This is all the more remarkable, given that the Lutheran and Reformed churches were separated for more than four hundred years precisely because of the controversy regarding the understanding of the Eucharist. Therefore, their ecclesial communion may rightly be termed an epochal ecumenical advance.

8.3 Baptismal recognition

In the »Magdeburg Declaration« from 2007, eleven Christian denominations represented in Germany agreed on the mutual recognition of their baptism. In this way they committed themselves, among other things, not to (re-)baptise Christians from one of these churches who joined their church, but to acknowledge their existing baptism. Thus, they accepted that the baptism in all these churches is valid according to their own standards, even though they do not have church communion. Insofar as baptism is a fundamental ecclesial act, they recognise by implication the religious quality of Christian fellowships distinct from their own. Therefore, the Magdeburg Declaration contains enormous ecclesiological potential, and its ecumenical significance is not yet apparent.

8.4 Theological agreement (»consensus ecumenism«)

From a Lutheran perspective, consensus on the understanding of the gospel and the proper administration of the sacraments is necessary for ecclesial communion. That means that the teaching of another church must in each case be recognised and accepted as a legitimate form of expression of the common

Christian faith. In other words, it has to be established that there is a sufficient degree of agreement on central questions of faith. This consensus has to be formulated in its content-related determination. Therefore, doctrinal discussions with the aim of joint declarations documenting the consensus achieved are a genuinely Lutheran ecumenical concern. A classic result of this procedure is the Leuenberg Agreement from 1973. The Joint Declaration on the Doctrine of Justification between Lutherans and Roman Catholics from 1999 follows the same approach, although it has not yet led to full church communion. To be sure, dialogues on doctrinal consensus alone cannot produce ecclesial communion. They are only meaningful if churches have already taken a road of common, confidence-building experiences leading to the expectation that the theological differences will not (or no longer) prove to be divisive. It is also clear that such discussions should not take place in a special ecumenical space which has little in common with the spiritual and theological life of the respective churches and is therefore ineffective. But if they are embedded within processes of increasing inter-church familiarity and trust, they remain an important and indispensable factor for reflecting, articulating and deepening the fellowship that has been reached.

8.5 Cooperation in social and charitable service and common civic involvement

Ecumenism is not only an issue for theologians. It is also not restricted to worship and the many other forms of religious communication. In point of fact, it is the charitable and social work which has turned out to be an important field for ecumenical witness, providing lively and visible proof of Christian fellowship, even though doctrinal differences have not been overcome and full communion of pulpit and altar not achieved. Ecumenical health and social service stations centres, railway station missions, joint projects of the Protestant »Diakonie« and the Catholic »Caritas«, reciprocal support in caring for the needy, etc., strengthen the bonds between the denominations and also send a strong signal to the outside world that in their charitable activities the Christian churches do not act in competition or parallel to one another, but in deliberate cooperation. This also applies to their common civic involvement, for example in refugee work or in their commitment for climate protection and ecological sustainability. Therefore, it is highly significant that on Reformation Day 2016 the leaders of the Lutheran World Federation together with Pope Francis not only attended a worship service in Lund, but also the signing of a Declaration of Intent in Malmö, by which the Lutheran World Service and Caritas International agreed to deepen their cooperation in all fields of global development work. This double event repeated in a condensed form the initiative which characterised the beginnings of the ecumenical movement, namely that the fellowship of the Christian churches proves itself not just in the search for theological consensus and common forms of worship (Faith and Order), but also in the joint testimony to life and love (Life and Work). Both dimensions belong together; they can enrich and strengthen one another.

Recently, another aspect has come increasingly into focus. In those states, mostly in the Northern world, which are ideologically neutral, the Christian churches are losing their social influence as a result of their dwindling membership figures. They are therefore making increasing attempts to join forces in defending Christian values and cultural traditions in the social and political sphere. Examples of this are the campaigns to ensure that Sunday remains a day of rest or to secure the presence of Christian symbols in public spaces, as well as joint initiatives for the protection of life and for the security and promotion of families.

Nevertheless, there are also limits to the common ground of the churches, and new differences are even coming to light. For example, the Protestant and Catholic churches in Germany have very diverse opinions on same-sex marriage, fertility treatment, state abortion laws, and so on, so that a common witness on these topics hardly seems possible. In addition, church members of the same denomination hold widely differing positions on such issues; on both sides, the official church statements do not correspond entirely to the convictions of their members. From a Protestant point of view, such ethical pluralism is not necessarily a deficiency, but rather an expression of the autonomy of conscience which is entrusted to, and expected of, individual believers. In modern secular societies, therefore, publicly articulated differences of judgment do not as such weaken the credibility of Christian witness. Indeed, a recently published joint Lutheran-Catholic paper entitled »God and Human Dignity« could prove ecumenically helpful in its attempt to reveal common basic principles and persuasions in ethical differences. Ecumenical statements on ethical questions would then serve the function of introducing these basic principles into social discourse without concealing or levelling out such differences. This way of dealing with conflicts of ethical judgment within and between churches – tolerant of ambiguity, but not indifferent – might possibly be considered exemplary for the secular sphere. This would benefit the influence of Christian witness more than a (merely supposed) consensus.

9. Outlook: A post-ecumenical age?

The present ecumenical climate is marked by trends running counter to one another. On the one hand, the distinctions between Christian denominations are decreasingly relevant to outsiders, to whom the classic theological controversies seem to be esoteric, incomprehensible disputes. Many Christians also see them in a different perspective in the face of the religious, cultural and political challenges that they are all sharing. On the other hand, there is increasing awareness of the intrinsic value of the differing denominational features. This need not be a contradiction to the ecumenical commitment. The phrase »ecumenism of profiles«, which was coined a few years ago, is intended to emphasise that denominational identity and ecumenical openness are not mutually exclusive, but complementary. The profile of one confession should not be exclusive, defining its identity at the expense of others.

We are not living in a post-ecumenical age. The achievements of ecumenism are irreversible. A return to the days of mutual and generalised condemnations, only seeing light in one's own denomination and darkness outside it, has become impossible. The mutual perception of churches has changed fundamentally in this respect. It is important to hang on to this revolutionary change, even if many ambitious hopes of Christians who are strongly committed to ecumenism have not been fulfilled. An amalgamation of major Christian churches has indeed never taken place; and many denominations are still a long way away from full church communion. Nevertheless, the impression of ecumenical stagnation is deceptive. In the view of Lutheran ecclesiology, organisational unification of the churches is not urgently required. It is not even desirable if it means reducing the wealth of confessional traditions. What is truly desirable and worthy of every effort, is interdenominational understanding which is so far-reaching that the highly conspicuous, and thus particularly symbolic, separation at the Lord's Table may be overcome, at least in the form of Eucharistic hospitality.

10. Literature

Michael Kappes / Ulrike Link-Wiezcorek / Sabine Pemsel-Maier / Oliver Schuegraf (eds.): Basiswissen Ökumene. Two volumes, Leipzig 2018.

Bernd Oberdorfer / Oliver Schuegraf (eds.): Sichtbare Einheit der Kirche in lutherischer Perspektive / Visible Unity of the Church from a Lutheran Perspective. Eine Studie des Ökumenischen Studienausschusses / A Study by the Ecumenical Study Committee. Bilingual edition (German/English), Leipzig 2017.

Dokumente wachsender Übereinstimmung. Sämtliche Berichte und Konsenstexte interkonfessioneller Gespräche auf Weltebene. Volumes 1–3 ed. by Harding Meyer / Damaskinos Pa-

PANDREOU / HANS JÖRG URBAN / LUKAS VISCHER, Paderborn/ Frankfurt a. M. 1991 (Vol. 1), 1992 (Vol. 2), 2003 (Vol. 3). Volume 4 ed. by JOHANNES OELDEMANN / FRIEDERIKE NÜSSEL / UWE SWARAT / ATHANASIOS VLETSIS, Paderborn/Leipzig 2012.

WOLFGANG BEINERT / ULRICH KÜHN: Ökumenische Dogmatik. Leipzig/Regensburg 2013.

EDMUND SCHLINK: Ökumenische Dogmatik. Grundzüge, Göttingen 1983.

Hendrik Munsonius

The Church and Its Law

An Introduction

1. Why is law necessary?

Actually, the church has nothing to do with law. Yet, the role of law in the church is not to be underestimated. When we say »actually«, it already signifies that it is worth taking a closer look. Strictly speaking, ecclesiastical law helps the church to be what it is supposed to be by nature. But what is the church? The Augsburg Confession, presented by Reformation rulers at the Diet of Augsburg in 1530, contains a description which is still important today. Alongside Martin Luther's Small Catechism, it is the most important confessional text of the Lutheran Church. Article 7 says of the church:

»We also teach that one holy Christian church must exist and remain at all times, and that this church is the gathering of all believers, among whom the gospel is purely preached and the holy sacraments are administered in accordance with the gospel. For this is sufficient for true unity of the Christian church, that the gospel is preached there in harmony according to a pure understanding of it and the sacraments are administered there according to God's Word.«

Thus, the Church is always to be found where the gospel is preached and the sacraments are administered. The church is therefore not primarily an organisation or institution, but a continuing practice. It exists by acting. And the law assists the church to fulfil these actions.

2. Church activity

The church is active in very many ways. For a better understanding, we may make the following classification:

First of all, there are those practices that are essential to the church and do not take place in other organisations: proclamation of the gospel by word and sacrament. Without these, one would not be able to speak of a church. They represent the *constitutive* activity of the church. The proclamation is publicly perceptible and is available to all in worship services. It takes place in the form of official acts at important stages in people's lives, such as baptism, confirmation, marriage and burial. And it takes place on a personal level, withdrawn from the public eye, in pastoral care. The act of proclamation is always intended to bring people to believe in the triune God, to help them to grow in faith and to enable them to live their lives in hope and confidence.

The activity of the church is not limited to proclamation. Faith has an impact on life. And so the churches and their members participate in many ways in people's lives and in society. This can be described as the *vital* action of the church. It is concerned with help in concrete need (social work, »Diakonie«), promotion of personality development (education) and participation in public life and political discourse (public responsibility). In these fields, the churches come into contact with other organisations that face the same tasks in their own way. And they are subject to the regulations and financing systems of the state and other public bodies.

The church needs resources for all its activities. Like any other organisation, it needs money, buildings, materials and above all people in order to perform its tasks. Obtaining and administering these resources is part of church *management*. This is not an end in itself, but is necessary for the purposes of constitutive and vital action. In this respect, the church is involved in many ways in economic contexts and is subject to the laws applying there.

When the church acts in so many different ways with so many people in various areas of life, it is obvious that this is not to be accomplished easily and free of conflicts. Activities have to be coordinated and conflicts settled in as many different ways as the church is involved.

For that reason, *church leadership* represents a particular dimension, which aims to shape and coordinate action in the three areas mentioned above. All those who are influential in shaping the church form a part of leadership. Parish councils, synods and governing boards assume a common responsibility for church action together with persons charged with certain offices. Special procedures apply, in which the participants engage in discussions and reach understandings. Decisions that are taken have a legal character: they make binding statements regarding the action of the church and the way in which it is to be implemented.

3. Law

The law is a particularly effective means of coordinating activities and settling conflicts, and is principally known in the form of state law.

Cooperation and conflict

Wherever people live together, it is inevitable that all of them are affected in all that they do by the things that the others do – particularly in a society based on the division of labour, where people get most of the goods and services they need from others. That is why it is normal for people to cooperate or to conflict with one another. In order to reach a fruitful agreement, it is necessary in both cases to clarify how cooperation may be achieved or conflicts resolved.

Such regulations cannot be re-negotiated for every new case. For one thing, the regulations for this negotiation would have to be agreed upon once more in their turn. On the other hand, the actions of people in a complex society based on the division of labour has an effect on many more people, who cannot be directly involved in the negotiation of such regulations. For this reason, standards are developed, meaning rules of behaviour that are required in the interests of fruitful cooperation of many people and of the non-violent termination of conflicts.

Rules of play, decency, morals, and law

Standards governing what may or may not be done can also apply in the form of rules of play, decency and morality. Whoever does not conform can be excluded from the game, loses the respect of society, or comes into conflict with their conscience. Legal standards have a higher claim to validity and are compulsorily enforced if necessary. Thus, everyone can expect legal standards to be respected by all and can base their own actions on this expectation.

If the law is not followed voluntarily, there are procedures to enforce the law against people's will, which are themselves legally regulated. Such a procedure can be initiated by any person who can validly claim that their rights have been infringed. Such personal rights might result from a contract, for example if someone demands payment of a purchase price or the use of a rented apartment. A dispute over the commitment to conduct a certain action can be clarified in a court.

In the case of commitment to other forms of conduct, the state can ensure that they are respected. By means of so-called administrative acts, state authorities can instruct someone to behave in a specific way. Accordingly, people who see themselves impaired in their rights by such action of the authorities can defend themselves by bringing a lawsuit.

Claim to validity of the law

The law's general claim to validity is based on the fact that the standards are considered to be legitimate. From a substantive point of view, the legitimacy of law is derived from its conformity to the guiding principles of law, in particular justice. This is illustrated by legal principles. For example, similar cases are to be treated in a similar way, people should be allowed to live their lives freely as long as they do not interfere with other people's freedom, and no one should be made to bear disproportionate burdens. Many of these legal principles have been formulated in constitutions, fundamental and human rights. They are therefore mandatory for the definition of all other norms and in the application of law. Whether or not they have been honoured can be reviewed in special court cases.

Beyond this substantive legitimacy of law, formal legitimacy (legality) is also necessary, that is to say, the way norms are created or established. When rights are formulated in the text of a law, it has to be done by specific bodies, in a specific form and by means of a specific procedure. In democracies, the enactment of a law requires an orderly consultation process and a parliamentary resolution followed by publication in an official journal or gazette. If no formal law exists with relation to a specific problem, court proceedings can determine in a given case what may be considered as lawful. This is referred to as case law. In such cases as well, correct competency and procedures must be observed.

4. Church law

The church participates in general legal life and is obliged to observe the prevailing laws. Within the framework of the laws that apply generally, it can organise its own affairs independently and pass its own laws. To start with, this church law is like any other law. It is generated, applied and enforced in a similar way. However, church law also differs substantially from other law on the grounds of its special function. It serves to realise the action of the church – that is to say, to ensure that what the church does is inherent to its purpose. The communication of the gospel is of central importance, so that people can come to faith and grow in it. This is something that cannot be identified and regulated by legal procedures. But church law is essential in order for it to happen. This is a problem which continually concerns all who formulate and use church law – whether lawyers or theologians.

The existence of church law is not least due to the fact that it helps the church to fulfil its true being – even if that appears at first sight to be a contradiction, since the communication of the gospel cannot be identified and regulated by law. The church is present wherever church activities take place. The decisive feature named by the Augsburg Confession (see above) is the gathering of believers, in which the gospel is taught and the sacraments administered. This is something which always takes place at a certain place and a certain time, with certain people taking part. Every congregation that gathers in this way is totally church. But it is never the total church. For the church is to be found wherever the church is active – irrespective of time and place. In this way the church is always quite specific, yet at the same time universal.

Because of this, every specific gathering (congregation) must strive to go beyond its temporal and spatial limitations. Preaching and other church activities should not only take place occasionally, every now and then, but at all places over and over again. That is why it is appropriate that people are commissioned to make sure that all this happens regularly and continuously. This overcomes temporal limitations. And it is also appropriate that every congregation understands itself as part of a larger community and strives to relate to other communities. Such relationships should not only occur occasionally on the basis of chance contacts, but subsist in the long term and over great distances.

If people are to be commissioned to work for a community in the long term, then reliable conditions are necessary. It has to be clear who is commissioning whom, which requirements are to be met, what obligations and rights are involved, how long an assignment is to last and how it can be terminated if necessary. These are questions which can be resolved by means of the law. The same applies for the permanent establishment of congregations and the relationship between different congregations. Legislative rules can serve to establish reliable structures and transparent procedures so that everyone can be sure of what they may expect from others and what is expected of them. The law thus helps to ensure that church activity takes place in a lasting and reliable way and that the relationship between each specific congregation and the universal church gains shape and takes practical form.

Distinction between the spiritual and the legal

Since the activities concerned are not within the reach of law, it is particularly important to pay attention to the distinction between what is spiritual and what is legal. In Reformation theology this was handled within the topic of the »two kingdoms doctrine«. According to this teaching, God works in two different ways (kingdoms) in this world: God's spiritual or »right-hand« kingdom concerns the life of faith. This government takes place through the proclamation of the Word and excludes the use of violence or compulsion. In the secular or »left-hand« kingdom, government is concerned with security and external peace and is exercised by law and, ultimately, by the power which is nowadays a monopoly of the state. The worldly government does not lead to piety, while the spiritual has no power with which to prevent evil.

This distinction between the two governments is also to be applied within the church. For the church is not only a spiritual but also a secular community, and it cannot do without worldly regulations. At the same time, the spiritual community develops and thrives in this worldly community.

Thus both »kingdoms« are at work in the church. Here again, a distinction must be made between the spiritual government, which is effected by the Word alone, and the external order, which must be maintained by means of law and sanctions. This prohibits any attempt to regulate preaching, which depends solely on the Word and the working of the Holy Spirit. That is the only way to work faith in people.

Ecclesiastical law has to protect the act of proclamation institutionally, creating the necessary conditions for staff, materials and organisation. This means that ecclesiastical law is on the one hand connected to the mandate of the church, while there is on the other hand considerable leeway for legal structure. Those responsible can formulate, maintain, alter or repeal church law. In many cases it is possible to follow a practical and pragmatic course, because it is not the purpose of church law to engender faith.

Unity of the spiritual and the legal

However, the distinction between the two »kingdoms« is not to be understood as meaning that there is no connection between them. Especially in the church struggle during the period of National Socialism it became clear that the external order of the church is to be distinguished from its message, but is not to be separated from it. This was established particularly clearly in the third thesis of the Theological Declaration of Barmen adopted in 1934 by representatives of Lutheran, Reformed and United churches at the Synod of the Confessional Church in order to oppose conforming the order of the church to National Socialist ideas.

»The Christian Church is the congregation of the brethren in which Jesus Christ acts presently as the Lord in Word and Sacrament through the Holy Spirit. As the church of pardoned sinners, it has to testify in the midst of a sinful world, with its faith as with its obedience, with its message as with its order, that it is solely his property, and that it lives and wants to live solely from his comfort and from his direction in the expectation of his appearance.

We reject the false doctrine, as though the church were permitted to abandon the form of its message and order to its own pleasure or to changes in prevailing ideological and political convictions.«

The order of the church must do justice to its message. Church law may not contradict what the church proclaims. It therefore derives its legitimacy not only from guiding principles such as righteousness, but especially from the church's teaching mission. Church law is legitimate as long as it helps to fulfil the mission of the church and is consistent with scripture and confession. For it is scripture and confession which define what the message of the church has to be.

The connection between message and order finds expression in the so-called »leadership dogma« which is codified in several church constitutions. Even when not expressed in a standardised form, this principle is meanwhile regarded as a fundamental component of church order. It states that all church leadership is performed both spiritually and legally in indispensable unity. However, this unity cannot be taken for granted. It must always be sought and realised anew whenever church leadership is active. It is always a spiritual matter whether and how rules and decisions are made in the church. Church law is therefore always subject to criticism and formation.

Order of life (»Lebensordnung«)

This special feature of church law is also evident in the »orders of life«, a type of regulation that is peculiar to the church. The orders of life are intended to provide far-reaching orientation for church action. They include sections on worship and church ceremonies, parish work, education, social service, and public responsibility. These are all areas that on the one hand require a certain legal order (because people work here together and can come into conflict with one another); on the other hand they are beyond the bounds of such an order (because they ultimately concern the communication of the gospel).

The orders of life reflect this on the basis of their special structure: each section deals first with the »perception of the situation« before elucidating »biblical foundations and theological orientation«, followed by »regulations«, which mostly relate to formal considerations, procedural rules and competences. The acting persons are thereby strengthened respectively in their responsibility. The competences are clear. And the horizon and insights which are to underlie decisions in each concrete case are also clear. Differences of opinion can be substantially settled on the basis of the order of life without insistence on a specific solution.

Church law as organisational law

Thus, church law serves the purpose of realising church activities; essential church action is beyond the bounds of legal regulation; and the connection between spiritual and legal leadership must always be maintained and continually regained. For these reasons church law consists for the most part of organisational law. It deals with the people involved in what the church does, with the structures in which they act and the procedures governing the understanding of church action and its implementation.

The regional churches in Germany benefit from the fact that they have a special status as a corporation under public law. They are not dependent on the legal forms of private law (such as the registered association), as is the case for other social organisations. In addition, they can organise themselves – like the state – in the forms of public law. This status is open to all religious communities. They can thus give themselves a legal form which corresponds better to their self-conception than would be possible under private law alone.

5. Persons

Basics

a) Universal priesthood

Church law is the order of church action, which involves all who belong to the church. According to the Protestant doctrine of the Universal Priesthood, all those baptised are equally authorised and commissioned to participate in the church's ministry. In the Protestant church there is no consecration as a prerequisite for special tasks. Martin Luther expressed this very vividly in 1520 in his tract »To the Christian Nobility of the German Nation«:

»All Christians are truly of the spiritual estate, and there is no difference among them, save of office alone. … Thus, we are all consecrated as priests by baptism. … Whatever issues from baptism may boast that it has been consecrated priest, bishop, and pope, although it does not beseem everyone to exercise these offices.«

Thus, through baptism, every Christian is called into direct communion with God and can turn to him in prayer. And all Christians should become priests to each other through witness to the gospel, intercession, pastoral care and confession.

b) Protestant official doctrine

The doctrine of Universal Priesthood does not exclude the formation of special ecclesiastical offices. Indeed, these offices exist for the sake of the Universal Priesthood, which is founded on baptism and faith. For this reason care has to be taken that the mission of the church is fulfilled, that is, that the gospel is proclaimed and the sacraments are administered in order to secure the development and growth of faith. To ensure the quantity and quality of these practices, it is appropriate to select and commission people who are suited and willing to perform them. In this context, Article 14 of the Augsburg Confession states:

»Of Ecclesiastical Order they teach that no one should publicly teach in the Church or administer the Sacraments unless he be regularly called.«

Anyone who is called into office »regularly« then does what most Christians do, but now »publicly«. That is, their actions are in principle valid for all people, and they act in the name of the church, the community that has commissioned them. Because of this public effect, a particular calling (ordination) is required as well as particular supervision (visitation) for this office, so that people also have to be commissioned to perform such ordinations and visitations. This is the classic function of bishops, which is often shared with others carrying responsibility.

c) Community of service

Not only for the office of public proclamation but also for all other ecclesiastical fields of action people must be found to take on the tasks involved. This happens in many different forms: as voluntary, full-time or part-time work, as employees, officials or ministers. In principle, all these forms of personnel can be found in any field of church work.

In order for them to work together, the idea of a community of service is fundamental. Everyone participating in the church's activities contributes to the fulfilment of the ecclesiastical mission. The individual activity occurs in a much larger context, in which people join together to enable the church of Jesus Christ to be experienced. All are called to employ their gifts and powers in common. They should trust one another to cooperate and seek agreement in the event of conflicts. This is often not easy. But just as every parish has to accept that it is not the whole church, so everyone who works in the church needs to see that they are doing so in fellowship with others. This community must not be neglected, but rather cultivated.

The law is not able to create trust, but only to make it possible. For this purpose, procedures are defined for taking decisions and dealing with conflicts, and the criteria for establishing such regulations are laid down. Every person who is affected should be involved in an appropriate manner. And those involved should know what is expected of them and what they may expect from others. The law serves this purpose by defining rights and duties. This makes the procedures transparent and dependable.

Legal relationships

a) Church membership

Before certain tasks can be assigned, it must be clarified who is involved in church activities at all. In special circumstances, these could also be people who are not members of the church. But as a rule, it is church members who act in the church. There are uniform rules for church membership. These state that all baptised persons of Evangelical confession living within the territory of a regional church are members of their local parish and their regional church. Compulsory membership is excluded, for baptism only takes place with the consent of those affected, which in the case of minors is given by the parents (as in other matters, too) or by other guardians. Whoever wishes to end their church membership is entitled to renounce it. All church members have the right to take part in church activities, they are supposed to participate in the life of the church and to take on tasks; and they are required to pay church tax in relation to their income, thus making church work possible.

Church membership is the legal relationship in which belonging to the church takes legal shape. When people leave the church, this legal relationship ends. Participation in church activities is then no longer possible (or only in a very limited way). Nonetheless, people who have left the church remain in a relationship to it. It is only the community of the church which is affected. Baptism has unceasing validity, and its promise remains in force. For that reason it is always possible to come back into the church later.

b) Volunteer service

All kinds of church work can in principle be performed on a voluntary basis. Volunteers can be found in Sunday schools, in church music, the preaching ministry, social service institutions and in administrative bodies from parish councils to church governing boards and the Council of the Evangelical Church in Germany. The overwhelming majority of church workers, totalling about 1.1 million people, are volunteers.

Voluntary work is done on a free-will basis and is unpaid – but it is nonetheless not in a legal vacuum. All voluntary tasks are performed on a contractual basis, whereby such a contract must not exist formally. The consent of those responsible is often sufficient if someone helps out at events or works in church groups. The contractual basis determines who and where a task is to be performed. The person or institution concerned may require the contract to be carried out precisely. Volunteers can expect to be granted protection and support and are entitled to reimbursement of the expenses incurred when fulfilling the assignment. For a number of voluntary church ministries it is appropriate to celebrate inauguration or termination in a church service.

c) Employment relationships

For permanent and time-consuming tasks requiring professional training, people are engaged on the basis of a contract of employment. In the established church there are about 200,000 employees, and about 450,000 work in social service (*Diakonie*). The working relationships are basically similar to those of other employers with the same rights and obligations regarding productivity, remuneration and care. For this reason, it is first and foremost the state employment regulations that apply.

The idea of a community of service, however, introduces certain modifications. Thus, the churches can make special demands upon the individual employees to ensure that their work is recognisable as church action. For example, church employees should normally also be church members. Such requirements are also covered by state law.

To resolve disputes over remuneration and working conditions, which are otherwise dealt with by means of industrial action (strike, lock-out), the churches have developed a special procedure, the so-called »Third Way«, which is applied in most regional churches. This means that such matters are decided in labour law commissions, consisting of an equal number of representatives of the employees and the employers. The voting rules ensure parity for both sides. If no agreement is reached, the dispute can be brought before an arbitration board. The Federal Labour Court has confirmed that these procedures entitle the churches to prohibit strikes in their institutions as long as employees' rights are adequately guaranteed.

Officials in a public corporation

Pastors and church officials are in an employment relation under public law, similar to state civil servants. The Evangelical Church in Germany has enacted laws governing the employment of church public servants and the rules for pastoral service. These persons are employed for life, which on the one hand ensures their stronger attachment to the church, and on the other hand gives the employees concerned greater security and freedom. This means that they can perform their service to the church reliably and independently. Pastors and church officials carry out their ministry with a high degree of personal responsibility. In particular, within the framework of the vows taken at ordination, pastors are not bound to any stipulations or directives when preaching. Even when they are not on duty, pastors and church officials are required to behave in accordance with their profession.

If the actions of pastors and church officials contradict their duties, disciplinary proceedings will be carried out. After the facts have been established, sanctions may be imposed ranging from a reprimand, a fine or a reduction in salary to dismissal from service. Disciplinary law is intended to safeguard the reputation of the church, the functionality of its service and an orderly conduct of official duties. The churches are not responsible for the punishment of criminal offences; that lies in the jurisdiction of the public prosecution and state courts.

A particular problem arises when statements are made in a sermon that are incompatible with scripture and confession. If the preacher is convinced of what has been preached, this does not amount to a culpable violation of duty, since a sermon should always reflect a personal conviction. The person is nonetheless not suited to public proclamation. For such cases a special procedure for doctrinal discipline exists. First of all, theological discussions take place in order to discern the doctrine represented and to what extent it contradicts scripture and confession. If the person concerned shows willingness and is prepared to abandon his or her doctrinal position, the investigation ends without further consequences. But if they insist on holding their divergent doctrine, then they are declared no longer fit for service to the church and dismissed from the ministry. However, there is no accusation of guilty conduct. Therefore follow-up care is offered, and a subsistence allowance may be paid. This procedure for doctrinal discipline should ensure that preaching is conducted authentically, but also in accordance with the church's confession and the gospel.

6. Structures

The regional churches mostly have a three-tiered structure: parish, »intermediate level« (church district, deanery …) and regional church. The church constitutions (ordinances) regulate the tasks of the respective levels, the bodies governing their actions and the way they cooperate with the other levels. The designations for organisations and persons are not standardised in these churches, but follow the regional traditions. Nonetheless, they have a great deal in common on the objective level of their regulations.

Structure of the regional churches

1) Parish
All Christians baptised into the Evangelical Church belong to the parish and are affiliated to it in a certain way. Usually they belong to the parish in which they live. However, one can also apply to belong to a different local parish or join a special group parish with people coming from a larger area. Larger

church agencies or diaconal institutions may also form their own community congregations, to which all those belong who live and work there.

The parish should put church life into practice locally as fully as possible. It is headed by the parish council (presbytery, church board, council of elders …) elected by the members at regular intervals (usually every six years). Other persons may be appointed to the council. The parish pastors automatically belong to it.

In the Lutheran tradition, particular importance is attached to the pastor's personal leadership responsibility alongside the parish council; that means that certain decisions of a particularly spiritual nature are taken by the pastor alone. The Reformed (and United) tradition, on the other hand, emphasises the joint leadership responsibility of pastor and presbytery.

2) Church District (intermediate level)

Parishes and church institutions of a particular region are associated in a church district (circuit, deanery, »intermediate level« …) to fulfil three tasks. Firstly, the district promotes and coordinates the work of the parishes. In addition, it is responsible for particular areas of church work, especially when these go beyond the scope or the capacity of individual congregations. And finally, it takes on administrative duties on behalf of the regional church administration, supervises the parishes and is responsible for the distribution of resources to the local churches.

The church district is led by a district synod (church assembly …), a board and a presiding pastor (superintendent, dean …). The synod is composed of representatives of the parishes, church institutions and agencies. It offers a platform for discussion and coordination and takes decisions on fundamental questions; it elects or appoints the members of other district bodies, draws up the budget, distributes resources, can found special facilities and carry out joint projects within the district. Normally there are committees to support this work. The district synod meets about four times a year for a one-day conference.

As a rule, the district board comprises the presiding pastor and the chairperson of the synod, their deputies and other elected persons. The head of administration usually participates in an advisory capacity. The board meetings are often monthly. The board is responsible for the continuous management of the district, prepares resolutions for the synod and implements them.

The presiding pastor is usually appointed in co-operation between the regional church and the district. That signifies that he or she is responsible to both of them for official duties: on the one hand care for supervision and visitation in the church district, on the other hand representation of the district publicly. Usually this pastor also serves as minister in a prominent parish, which also has to be consulted for the appointment.

3) Regional church

The regional church includes all the parishes, church districts and agencies in a larger area. Today, there are 20 regional churches in Germany numbering between 46,000 and 2.9 million members. The areas of the regional churches have their origin in the former dominions and principalities in Germany, but they did not follow the changes that took place after the separation of church and state; during the twentieth century various alterations in the territorial structures of the churches were made.

On a legal level, the regional church is decisive. This is where most of the laws are passed, and here the decision is taken as to which legislation of other levels in the regional church is valid. As a rule, the leadership of the regional churches comprises four bodies:

The Synod (»Kirchentag« …) forms the largest institution. It represents the regional church in its diversity and entirety. The members of the Synod are representatives elected from the church districts and – where appropriate – from other fields of church work, people specially appointed, and in some cases representatives of other governing bodies. Its tasks include legislation, budgetary decisions, appointments to other governing bodies and consultation on all important issues of church life.

The office of Bishop was already established in the Ancient Church, which assigned ecclesiastical supervision and leadership in a particular area to individual clergymen. Their duties consisted in particular in the ordination of the pastors and the visitation of the congregations. This function has continued to be performed by special officials in the Reformation churches as well. In the ministry of the Bishop the emphasis lies in the proclamation, so that it has above all a communicative function. In addition, bishops (church president, president …) participate in the leadership activities of other governing boards as chairperson, full member or with speaker's rights. The larger regional churches have additional regional bishops (regional superintendent, provost …) who perform episcopal functions for a certain area (»Sprengel«) within the regional church and act in conjunction with its Bishop.

No regional church can manage without a central administration (Church Office, chancery, consistory …), which prepares and implements the decisions of the other governing bodies and deals with day-to-day business. Mainly theologians, lawyers and experts on finance and administration work together here. The administrative offices are divided into operational areas (department, secretariat, unit …) headed by a directive and representative board. As in other administrations, internal service operation is managed by organisational plans and rules of procedure.

The Church Council (church government, church senate …) is the coordinating centre of the governing bodies. It is responsible for the day-to-day management of the regional church and is responsible for the unity of church action. It often forms the institutional bond between the other governing bodies which are represented in it. It takes all the important decisions that are not the prerogative of the Synod – in particular staff appointments. It has instruction rights over the administration, and the right of initiative in the Synod.

The relationship between the governing bodies is regulated differently in the various regional churches. According to the separation model, the Synod stands on the one side, the Bishop, Church Council and Church Office on the other. They have no common staff, and their tasks and competencies are carefully delineated. In the unified model, all church leadership is concentrated in the Synod; the executive committee of the Synod is identical with the church leadership and closely connected with the administration. The responsibilities are not sharply divided from one another. The presiding pastor also chairs the Synod, the Church Council and the Church Office. In mixed models, the Church Council plays a particular role in connecting the various institutions, clarifying their individual responsibilities and integrating all directive action. In the long run, it can be seen that the different leadership models are coming closer to one another in order to find optimal solutions.

Associations of regional churches

1) Evangelical Church in Germany (EKD)
The regional churches have merged in the Evangelical Church in Germany (EKD). The tasks of the EKD are defined in Article 6 of its Basic Regulation:

»Article 6.
(1) The Evangelical Church in Germany strives to strengthen and deepen the communion among the member churches, helps them to fulfil their ministry and promotes the exchange of their powers and resources.
(2) It aims to ensure that the member churches proceed according to the same principles in essential matters of ecclesiastical life and action, so long as their confession allows.«

The following articles state that the EKD can support institutions and tasks that are of importance to the whole church, make suggestions to the regional churches and lay down guidelines. It may also pass church laws affecting the regional churches if they approve them.

The EKD is governed by the Synod, the Council, and the Church Conference. The Synod consists of 100 members elected by the synods of the regional churches and 20 persons appointed by the Council. The Council comprises the President of the Synod and fourteen further members elected jointly by the Synod and the Church Conference. The Chairperson of the Council is one of its members proposed by the Council and selected by the Synod. This must not necessarily be a bishop, although this has in fact always been the case so far. The Church Conference is formed of representatives delegated by the governing boards of the member churches. The governing bodies of the EKD are assisted by the Church Office, which also conducts the day-to-day administration.

2) United Evangelical Lutheran Church of Germany (VELKD)
Within the EKD, the Lutheran regional churches (with the exception of Oldenburg and Württemberg) have joined together to form the United Evangelical Lutheran Church of Germany (VELKD). According to Article 1 of its constitution, it considers itself to be a »union of Evangelical Lutheran churches (member churches), which are bound to this confession in their preaching and administration of the sacraments as well as in their order, leadership and management and in the entire action of the church«. The basic confessions are in particular the Augsburg Confession of 1530 and Martin Luther's Small Catechism.

The VELKD is supposed to promote the unity of this United Church, to commit itself to Lutheran teaching, to support the Lutheran diaspora and Lutheran agencies. It represents its affiliated Lutheran churches in public and in ecumenical relations. It can enact church laws affecting the member churches; their approval is not mandatory, but is nonetheless always obtained.

The governing bodies of the VELKD are the Bishops' Conference and the Presiding Bishop, the General Synod and the Church Council. The Bishops' Conference consists of the bishops of the member churches and other church leaders delegated by them. The Presiding Bishop is elected by the General Synod for three years, is Chairperson of the Church Council and the Bishops' Conference, represents the VELKD and has as »principal clergy« the right to preach from all the pulpits within the VELKD. The General Synod is the legislative body of the VELKD. It consists of 50 members elected by the synods of the member churches of the VELKD or appointed by the Presiding Bishop. The Church Council is responsible for all the issues not dealt with by the Bishops' Conference or the General Synod. It consists of the Presiding Bishop, his or her deputy, one further member of the Bishops' Conference, the President of the General Synod and nine other members. The work is supported by the Lutheran Church Office in the Church Office of the EKD.

3) Union of Evangelical Churches in the Evangelical Church in Germany (UEK)

In the Union of Evangelical Churches in the Evangelical Church in Germany (UEK), twelve regional churches of various confessions have come together to »promote what they have in common in significant areas of church life and action and thus strengthen the unity of the Evangelical Church in Germany« (Article 1 of the Constitution of the UEK). In its work, the UEK focuses on theological and liturgical issues and on the promotion of European and ecumenical relations. The UEK enacts laws for its member churches if they approve them.

The governing bodies of the UEK are the Plenary Conference and the Presidium. The Plenary Conference comprises all members of the Synod and the Church Conference of the EKD who come from the UEK member churches. It takes all basic decisions. The Presidium is responsible for the day-to-day management. It consists of the Chairperson of the Plenary Conference and two deputies as well as one member from each member church and the head of the Church Office. The theological and legal committees are standing committees. The work is supported by the Church Office of the UEK in the Church Office of the EKD.

Cooperation – Regionalisation

It is the case that church organisations are not an end unto themselves. They exist in order to ensure that vital and constitutive church action can take place. Therefore, it is always necessary to ask what is the best possible form for this purpose. The church lives in, but not on its structures. Since all organisation in the church has a serving capacity, no organisational form is unalterable. Under different external conditions and circumstances changes may well be advisable.

On a closer look, it turns out that simple and uniform solutions are not possible. For some fields of action small organisations are helpful, for others they should be larger. Thus, it may be advantageous for the contact between pastors and church members if the congregation is not too large. On the other hand, if there are only a few children living in the parish and attending Sunday School, that lessens the enjoyment. And many parishes are too small to be able to afford their own office.

For these reasons many churches are now trying to overcome the limitations of traditional parish boundaries and to find suitable forms for regional cooperation. If individual parishes cannot perform certain tasks alone, they can join forces in working groups and associations. Then certain tasks are performed together, and joint committees are formed that can make all the necessary decisions. However, the cooperation between the various fields of action should not be disturbed by dividing them up between different organisations. It is therefore always necessary to compromise. Because the church does not prescribe a specific form of organisation according to Protestant understanding, but merely wishes to administer the gospel in words and deeds, there is great scope for freedom in finding and developing appropriate forms for this purpose.

7. Procedures

Administration

Church law regulates the actions of the church, which are diverse and involve many people in many different ways. In order to make sure that the church is actually able to fulfil its mission, decisions repeatedly have to be taken with more or less far-reaching consequences. Wherever individual cases are concerned, one speaks of administrative procedures, even if there are large numbers of such cases. It is always a question of making the right (or at least the appropriate) decision in the specific instance. Decisions do not just happen of their own accord; they have to be taken by means of certain procedures. Therefore it is necessary to clarify by whom and how they are taken and how other people can be allowed to participate.

Procedural rules exist for all fields of church activity. They concern management – from parish church councils and ministries to district councils and the regional Church Office. This is to ensure that all those involved or affected are adequately taken into account before decisions are taken. That is why the invitation to meetings must be made in good time and an agenda drawn up. That is why those affected have to be heard before anything is decided on their behalf. And to make decisions effective, it has to be clearly established who is responsible for their subsequent implementation. In all cases, regulations are intended to protect those who are absent at the time and unable to influence the proceedings.

Legislation

Church law serves the purpose of fulfilling the church's mission of witnessing to the gospel in word and deed. This can only happen in the respective concrete situations of life. As life conditions change, so church action has to develop. Therefore, church law, which orders ecclesiastical action, is never unalterable, but subject to criticism and change. A legal norm only applies as long as it is not changed or repealed by a legislative act.

Legislation takes place when the competent body adopts a legal act according to the prescribed procedure and publishes it in the correct form. Legislation takes place above all in the synods, which pass church laws. Such laws can be proposed by members of the Synod or by the Church Council (right of initiative). Within the framework of the laws, the authorities and administrations of the regional churches can also issue legal and administrative regulations. All laws and regulations are published in official church journals and compiled in collections of laws for practical use.

Church law can change, but it is not arbitrary. It always takes shape in the context of scripture and confession. No legal norms can be derived directly from the Bible and confessional writings. But these texts provide essential guidance when deciding which actions are appropriate for the church, and therefore what church laws are suitable and correspond to its nature. What that means specifically for church law always requires discussion.

In the legislative process, various provisions have been made to safeguard the commitment to scripture and confession. For example, the voting on a resolution is suspended when certain persons maintain that a rule of law violates scripture and confession. This objection must first be discussed and removed before a legal norm can be put into effect. In this way, it is possible to respect the connection between the Christian message and legal order which was emphasised by the Barmen Theological Declaration.

Supervision

Church law should provide reliable orientation for all who participate in the church's activities. This will only succeed if adherence to the norms is ensured. In addition, those involved often need advice and support in order to comply with all relevant provisions of church and state law. This is the role played by supervision, as practised by the regional churches and church districts.

This occurs in a many different ways. First of all, the supervisory authorities can provide information and advice in the interests of good results. When it comes to decisions that are more complex and have far-reaching implications, approval can be made dependent on a review of the impending decision by experts. Should it happen that unlawful decisions have been taken, they can be repealed. And if a committee is unwilling or unable to do its job, the supervisory body must take direct action or delegate it to others. In the worst case, persons may be deprived of their office or a committee disbanded if there is obviously no prospect of constructive work in the long term.

Visitation

One supervisory procedure which is peculiar to the church is visitation. This has been one of the bishops' duties since time immemorial and is nowadays often carried out by the presiding pastors of the church district (superintendent, dean) together with visitation commissions. It consists of a visit to parishes and church institutions with the aim of gaining a comprehensive picture of church life. Before a parish is visited it usually prepares a report on its situation. During the visitation, talks are held with pastors, committees, church workers and groups. The institutions and church properties are inspected and paperwork checked. One aspect of the visitation is always a worship service, and usually a congregational assembly is held.

The visitors discuss what they have learned immediately with the persons responsible in the parish and others affected. After the visit, the visitator draws up a report for the church leadership, and the parish is entitled to make its own comments. In addition, suggestions for future work in the parish can be offered, proposals issued or objectives agreed. The purpose of the visitation is to promote the life of the local congregations and to give church leadership an impression of church life in its territory. It serves to connect the individual parishes with the broader ecclesiastical situation.

Finally, order in the church is guaranteed by ecclesiastical jurisdiction. The ecclesiastical courts serve to decide on the interpretation and application of church law, that is to say, to determine whether a particular action in the church corresponds to what has been generally and bindingly decided concerning church affairs. In this way, conflicts can be settled by an orderly procedure in a reliable way. The organisation and procedures of the church courts are based on the state model. In practice, however, they are bound to the specific legislation of the church and ultimately to scripture and confession – as are all others who make decisions on, or participate in, the dealings of the church. The fact that the church has its own courts does not preclude state courts having jurisdiction over ecclesiastical matters as far as they concern general state law.

8. Literature

Heinrich de Wall / Stefan Muckel: Kirchenrecht. Ein Studienbuch, München 5th edition, 2017.

Martin Honecker: Evangelisches Kirchenrecht. Eine Einführung in die theologischen Grundlagen, Göttingen 2009.

Christoph Link: Kirchliche Rechtsgeschichte. Kirche, Staat und Recht in der europäischen Geschichte von den Anfängen bis ins 21. Jahrhundert, München 3rd edition, 2017.

Hendrik Munsonius: Evangelisches Kirchenrecht. Grundlagen und Grundzüge, Tübingen 2015.

Vereinigte Ev.-Luth. Kirche Deutschlands (ed.): Leitlinien kirch-

lichen Lebens. Handreichung für eine kirchliche Lebensordnung, Gütersloh 2003.
The collections of laws of most regional churches are to be found under www.fis-kirchenrecht.de.

Authors

Pastor Dr. theol. habil. Martin Kumlehn is lecturer and Associate Professor of Practical Theology at the Humboldt-University Berlin.

Dr. theol. h. c. Christian Lehnert is a writer and theologian, and also Executive Secretary of the VELKD Institute for Liturgical Science in Leipzig since 2011.

Oberkirchenrat Dr. jur. Hendrik Munsonius, Master of Theology (Marburg University), is a consultant at the EKD Institute for Church Law in Göttingen.

Dr. theol. Bernd Oberdorfer, is Professor of Systematic Theology and Contemporary Theological Issues at the University of Augsburg, Chairperson of the Commission on Ecumenical Studies of the German National Committee of the Lutheran World Federation (GNC/LWF), member of the LWF Council and the Faith and Order Commission of the World Council of Churches.

Dr. theol. Michael Roth is Professor of Systematic Theology and Social Ethics at the Johannes Gutenberg University, Mainz.

Editors

Florian Hübner is Press Secretary and Church Executive for Public Relations and World Service at the German National Committee of the Lutheran World Federation (GNC/LWF).

Oberkirchenrätin Rev. Henrike Müller is Press Secretary and Church Executive for Public Relations of the United Evangelical Lutheran Church of Germany (VELKD).